Copyright © 2004 Susan Scheewe Publications Inc.
13435 N.E. Whitaker Way - Portland, Or. 97230
PH(503)254-9100 Fax (503)252-9508
PRINTED IN THE USA
e-mail: scheewepub@aol.com
web site: http://www.painting-books.com

Dedication

This first book, and all the books in the future, will be dedicated first and always to my best friend and the love of my life, Ron. We have been married for 21 years. He has put up with my mood swings, late dinners, and a messy house☺. Thank you, Ron, for all the support and love. I couldn't have accomplished my painting dreams without you!

Ron and I have raised three boys. Let me try and paint a perfect picture of each of them in a few short sentences.

Paul (age 27)….single, very handsome, hard worker, and has a love for adventure. Cody (age 17)….good-looking, intelligent, sharp sense of humor and a brutally honest teenager! Mason (age 8)... tall for his age, cute as a button, and has a love for baseball and soccer and ……he is still young enough to think everything I paint is perfect☺.

Dad and Mom…thank you for giving me my hidden talent of design and painting. I have always felt your love and support in all aspects of my life. You both have been a constant blessing in my life. I love you.

To my brother Rod and my sister Barb….through your hardships and turmoil, I have learned to appreciate every day to it's fullest!

There are so many people that I need to thank, and if I tried, I would unintentionally miss someone. So, I'm playing it safe and writing this generically but with sincere thanks. A big hug and thank you to Donna Dewberry who has given me the confidence to pursue my own dreams. Thank you to all my friends at work…you have been an enormous amount of support. To all my internet buddies (far too many to mention by name, but you know who you are!). You always put a smile on my face and make me feel so special…thank you. My students…both past and present….thank you for sharing the love of painting with me. Your enthusiasm and eagerness to learn is what made our time together so special.

Last, but not least,….thank you Sue Scheewe and staff for all your guidance and patience during the process of pulling this book together. You have made this journey a fun and exciting experience.

Introduction

Hmmm….this is the hard part. I am……… never mind…...you don't need to know my age....lol (laughing out loud). I've been painting for 15+ years. I believe my parents had a lot to do with my love of color and design. I remember when I was small that there were always coloring books and new crayons to be had. Of course, I had to take the wrappers off of each and every one of them and line them up in a row. Heaven forbid if I broke one…broken crayons just didn't work! It's funny the things you remember as time goes by☺.

I have taken several classes from the "big brushes". After much trial and error, I fell into my own style of painting. I had special painting buddies that gave me that extra little "push" to pull
a book together. Thank you, Allison Tudor and Pam Bialas for your friendship and confidence in me.

I've worked very hard trying to make this book fun and easy to follow. The directions are in the order that I painted the project and I have inserted little tips that I thought would be helpful instead of having to decipher color codes and flipping back and forth for painting directions.

I've not had formal training in the art industry. I just paint what I love and try to share that love of painting with others. I've taught many, many students in my home studio that Ron built for me. I have loved every minute of teaching!

I hope this book finds you with a happy heart and paint brush in hand. Thank you for sharing my first book. Big hugs to all…

All rights reserved under the Pan American International Copyright conventions. No part of this publication may be reproduced or utilized in any form or by any mechanical or electronic means, including photocopying, photographing, computer scanning or any information storage and retrieval system without permission from the publisher.

The information in this book is presented in good faith: however, no warranty is given nor are results guaranteed. Susan Scheewe Publications Inc. disclaims any liability for untoward results. Patterns may only be hand traced for personal use or teaching only. Not for commercial reproduction or mass marketing such as the gift industry. The designs in this book are protected by copyright; however, you may use the designs for your personal use or to sell in local craft markets.

Morning Glory - Thermometer

Palette - DecoArt Americana

Hi-Lite Flesh	Light Mocha	Brush'n Blend	Wild Orchid
Pansy Lavender	Emperor's Gold	Titanium White	Mint Julep Green
Avocado	Midnight Blue	Soft Lilac	Williamsburg Blue
Black/Green	Dioxazine Purple		

Brushes - Loew Cornell

#10 Flat   #3 Round   3/8" Angular Shader   #10/0 Liner

Other Supplies

Graphite Paper   Stylus
Fine Sandpaper   Tack Cloth
Old Toothbrush   Large Sponge Brush
Wood Thermometer (Bill Chiles)   J.W. Wipe on Varnish

Prep

Use the large sponge brush and basecoat the wood thermometer with **Hi-Lite Flesh**. Sand lightly and then use tack cloth.

Use an old toothbrush and thinned down **Emperor's Gold** and sprinkle the project. *(Tip: Do not water the paint too much...you will get big blobs of paint.)*

Use the #10 flat and **Emperor's Gold** and paint around the edges and inside where the thermometer sits. Let dry thoroughly.

If you choose to use the patterns, now is the time to trace them on. Use the graphite paper and the stylus to trace pattern on the wood. *(Tip: Use just enough pressure to transfer the pattern...you don't want to see transfer marks after you are finished with this project!)*

Morning Glories - Refer to Morning Glory Worksheet

I have painted two purple morning glories that look very similar. Base all three Morning Glories with **Soft Lilac** using either the flat brush or the angle brush. Let dry.

Use your angle brush with **Hi-Lite Flesh** on the tip and **Brush n' Blend** on the heel. Blend very well on your palette before you paint the "smile" on your Morning Glories. Paint all three "smiles" on the Morning Glories.

(Tip: Before we paint any further, I would like to warn you....these Morning Glories go through an UGLY stage.....don't panic!)

Purple Morning Glories – Refer to Morning Glory Worksheet

I used a flicking motion to achieve the thin lines in the Morning Glories. Use your #3 round, mix a little **Brush n' Blend** with **Wild Orchid** and "flick" all the way around the flower. *(Tip: Flatten your round brush in the paint and blending gel. Start on the outside of your flower, start on chisel edge and "flick" toward the middle of the flower.)* Let Dry.

Morning Glory - Thermometer - Purple Morning Glories continued

Do this same technique with **Pansy Lavender** and then with **Williamsburg Blue**.
(Tip: "Flick" in various spots…not all the way around the flower.)

This step will make the Morning Glory finally look like it is suppose too! Using your angle brush, dip the tip in **Dioxazine Purple** and **Brush n' Blend** on the heel. Blend well before painting on your surface. Laying the brush almost horizontally, make small strokes all the way around the Morning Glory following the same shape of the flower. At this point also shade on both sides of the neck of the flower. Use the chisel edge and pull in a few lines on the neck.

Use your liner and thinned down **Hi-Lite Flesh** and pull thin lines from the outside in
(Tip: I usually pull these little lines in where the flower comes to a point.)

Use thinned down **Emperor's Gold** and pull stamens from the inside out. Use your stylus and put little dots in the smile.

Blue Morning Glory - Refer to Morning Glory Worksheet

You have already basecoated and put the smile in at this point. Flick all the way around with **Williamsburg Blue**. Let dry. Flick with **Wild Orchid**. Let dry. Shade all the way around with **Midnight Blue**. Follow the steps above and paint this blue Morning Glory.

Leaves - Refer to Leaf Worksheet

Base the leaves with **Avocado** and **Black Green**.

On this project I used **Mint Julep Green** to pull a vein from one end to the other end of the leaf with the chisel edge of my 3/8" angular brush. While the vein is wet, pull down some "feathers".

Use the same brush and pull in **Mint Julep Green** from the outside of the leaf toward the middle and let dry.

Pull in **Wild Orchid** from the outside in (just like you did with the **Mint Julep Green**).

Use your liner and mix **Titanium White** and **Mint Julep Green** together and add veins to your leaf. *(Tip: Thin down this paint mixture before painting veins.)*

Use your liner and pull from the outside in and only on one side with **Emperor's Gold**. I do not thin the paint when I paint these little accents on the leaf.

White Filler Flowers - Refer to Filler Flower Worksheet

I used a #3 round with **Titanium White**. Touch and pull in various spots.

Finishing

Let your piece dry completely and seal with J.W. Wipe-On Varnish. I use a damp cloth and varnish to seal my piece. *(Tip: Keep your damp used cloth in a ziplock bag. Use it over and over.)*

Pattern on Pullout

Morning Glory - Mailbox

Palette - DecoArt Americana

Hi-Lite Flesh	Avocado	Pansy Lavender	Titanium White
Mint Julep Green	Soft Lilac	Black/Green	Dioxazine Purple
Brush'n Blend	Faux Glazing Medium		

Brushes - Loew Cornell

5/8", 1/2" Angular   #10/0 Liner   #3 Round   Large Soft Brush

Other Supplies

Graphite Paper   Fine Block Sander
Tack Cloth   Sea Sponge
Stylus   Rubbing Alcohol
J.W. Exterior Varnish   Metal Mailboxes (Home Depot or Lowes)

Prep

Use rubbing alcohol and a clean cloth to remove any oils or dirt on the mailbox. Use a sea sponge and lightly tap in **Hi-Lite Flesh** and **Soft Lilac**. Cover the entire surface. *(Tip: Wet the sponge and then wrap in a towel to remove all water.)* Let dry.

If you choose to use the patterns, now is the time to trace them on. Use the graphite paper and the Stylus to trace pattern on the mailbox.

Morning Glories - Refer to Morning Glory Worksheet

Base in all Morning Glories with **Soft Lilac** using one of the angle brushes. Let dry.

Paint in the "smiles" using the 5/8" angle brush. With **Hi-Lite Flesh** on the tip and **Brush n' Blend** on the heel paint the smiles. Refer to Morning Glory Worksheet.

(Tip: Before we paint any further, I would like to warn you....these Morning Glories go through an UGLY stage.....don't panic!)

Morning Glories - Refer to Morning Glories Worksheet

I used a flicking motion to achieve the thin lines in the Morning Glories. Use your #3 round, mix a little **Brush n' Blend** with **Pansy Lavendar** and "flick" all the way around the flower. (Tip: Flatten your round brush in the paint and blending gel. Start on the outside of your flower, start on chisel edge and "flick" toward the middle of the flower.)

Do this same technique with **Dioxazine Purple**. (Tip: "Flick" in various spots…not all the way around the flower.)

This step will make the Morning Glory finally look like it is suppose too! Use your 5/8" angle brush, dip the tip in **Dioxazine Purple** and **Brush n' Blend** on the heel. Blend well before painting on your surface. Laying the brush almost horizontally, make small strokes all the way around the Morning Glory following the same shape of the flower. At this point also shade on both sides of the neck of the flower. Use the chisel edge and pull in a few lines on the neck.

Morning Glory - Mailbox continued

Use your liner and thinned down **Hi-Lite Flesh** and pull thin lines from the outside in (I usually pull these little lines in where the flower comes to a point.)

Use thinned down **Emperor's Gold** and pull stamens from the inside out. Use your Stylus and put little dots in the smile.

Ribbons - Refer to Ribbon Worksheet

Mix one part **Soft Lilac** with four parts Faux Glazing Medium. *(Tip: The glaze will make the ribbon transparent, so adjust to your liking.)* Use the 5/8" angular brush and paint in the ribbons.

Shade with **Pansy Lavendar** and highlight with **Titanium White**. See Ribbon Worksheet.

Leaves - Refer to Leaf Worksheet

These leaves are based with **Avocado** and **Black Green**.

Use **Mint Julep Green** to pull a vein from one end to the other end of the leaf. Use the edge of a 1/2" angular brush. While the vein is wet, pull down some "feathers".

Use the same brush and pull in **Mint Julep Green** from the outside in and let dry.

Use your liner and mix **Titanium White** and **Mint Julep Green** together and add veins to your leaf.

Use your liner and pull from the outside in and only on one side with **Emperor's Gold**. I do not thin the paint when I paint these little accents on the leaf.

Curlicues

Use thinned **Avocado** and your liner brush. Roll the brush in the mixture and start making small circles and then slowly lower the brush to the surface. *(Tip: Stay on the very tip of the brush...this will help make very thin curlicues.)*

Finishing

Let your piece dry completely and seal with J.W. Exterior Varnish (Gloss). I use a large soft brush to put this varnish on. I paint in one direction...let dry...and paint the other direction. I love the texture that the brush leaves☺. I put at least three coats of varnish on.

Pattern on Pullout

Morning Glory - Watering Can

Palette - DecoArt Americana

Hi-Lite Flesh	Pansy Lavender	Williamsburg Blue	Wild Orchid
Mint Julep Green	Brush'n Blend	Titanium White	Soft Lilac
Emperor's Gold	Midnight Blue	Dioxazine Purple	Black Green
Avocado	Faux Glazing Medium		

Brushes - Loew Cornell

#12, #10 Flat   1/2", 5/8" Angular   #3 Round   #10/0 Liner

Other Supplies

Tack Cloth
J.W. Wipe-On Varnish
Metal Watering Can (WalMart)
Stylus

Prep

No prep on this piece…yippee! I found this watering can already crackled at WalMart! Just wipe with tack cloth and trace pattern.

(Tip: Before we paint any further, I would like to warn you….these Morning Glories go through an UGLY stage at first…don't panic)!

Morning Glories - Basecoating - Refer to Morning Glories Worksheet

Base all three Morning Glories with **Soft Lilac** using your flat or angle brushes. Use your 1/2" angle brush with **Hi-Lite Flesh** on the tip and Brush n'Blend on the heel. Blend very well on your palette before you paint the "smile" on your Morning Glories. Paint all three "smiles" and let dry.

Purple Morning Glories - Refer to Morning Glories Worksheet

I used a flicking motion to achieve the thin lines in the Morning Glories. Use your #3 round, mix a little **Brush n' Blend** with **Wild Orchid** and "flick" all the way around the flower. (*Tip: Flatten your round brush in the paint mixture. Start on the outside of your flower, start on chisel edge and "flick" toward the middle of the flower.*)

Do this same technique with **Pansy Lavender** and then with **Williamsburg Blue**.
(*Tip: "Flick" in various spots…not all the way around the flower.*)

This step pulls all the flicks together…it's a fun step☺. Use your 1/2" or the 5/8" angle brush, dip the tip in **Dioxazine Purple** and **Brush n' Blend** on the heel. Blend well before painting on your surface. Laying the brush almost horizontally, make small strokes all the way around the Morning Glory following the shape of the flower. At this point, also shade on both sides of the neck of the flower. Use the chisel edge and pull in a few lines on the neck.

If you want the little "tips" on your flowers, this is the time to paint them in. Use thinned **Dioxazine Purple** and your liner brush.

Morning Glory - Watering Can - Purple Morning Glories continued
Use your liner and thinned down **Hi-Lite Flesh** and pull thin lines from the outside in *(Tip: I usually pull these little lines in where the flower comes to a point.)*

Use thinned down **Emperor's Gold** and pull stamens from the inside out. Use your stylus and put little dots in the smile.

Blue Morning Glory
You have already basecoated and put the smile in at this point. Flick all the way around with **Williamsburg Blue**. Flick with **Wild Orchid** and shade all the way around with **Midnight Blue**. Complete as you did with the Purple Morning Glories.

Leaves-Refer to Leaf Worksheet
These leaves were based with **Avocado** and **Black Green**. I used **Mint Julep Green** to pull a vein from one end to the other end of leaf with the chisel edge of my 1/2" angular brush. While the vein is wet, pull in some "feathers".

Use the same brush and pull in **Mint Julep Green** from the outside in and let dry.

Pull in **Wild Orchid** from the outside in (just like you did with the **Mint Julep Green**).

Use a thin mixture of **Titanium White** and **Mint Julep Green** and add veins to your leaf.

Use your liner and pull from the outside in and only on one side with **Emperor's Gold**. I do not thin the paint when I paint these little accents on the leaf.

Ribbon-Refer to Ribbon Worksheet
Mix one part **Wild Orchid** with four parts **Faux Glazing Medium**. (Tip: The glaze will make the ribbon transparent, so adjust the color to your liking.) I used a 5/8" angular shader for my ribbon, but you can get the same results from a flat brush. Always start on chisel edge, press the bristles to the side, pull back up on chisel edge.

Here is an easy way to remember what is shaded and what is highlighted. If it is a skinny part of the ribbon...shade with **Pansy Lavender**. If it is the fat part of the ribbon...highlight with **Titanium White**.

Filler Flowers-Refer to Filler Flower Worksheet
I used a #3 round with **Titanium White**. I just touched and pulled in various areas.

Curlicues
Use thinned **Avocado** and a liner brush. Roll the brush in the mixture and start making small circles and then slowly lower the brush to the surface. *(Tip: Stay on the very tip of the brush...this will help makes very thin curlicues.)*

Finishing
Use your #10 or #12 flat brush and paint the solid areas. I used **Wild Orchid** on the handle, bottom portion, top rim and end of spout.

Morning Glory - Watering Can - Finishing continued

Gold Edging - Use **Emperor's Gold**. *(Tip: I use my finger ☺. I have found I have more control with my finger than I do with a brush.)*

Let your piece dry completely and seal with J.W. Wipe-On Varnish. I pour a little varnish on a damp cloth and gently rub over my piece. *(Tip: Store the damp cloth in a ziplock bag and use many, many times.)*

Morning Glory - Watering Can

Morning Glory

Use 3/8" angular brush. Base with Soft Lilac. Paint smile with Hi-Lite Flesh on tip and brush n' blend on heel.

Use Wild Orchid and a #3 round brush. Stand on chisel edge and flick toward the middle of the flower. Follow in the shape of the flower.

Using Pansy Lavender and a second color shade under smile and down the sides of the neck.

Flick a small amount of Dioxazine Purple. Shade all around the edges using Dioxazine Purple on tip and brush n' blend on heel. Use liner and thinned Dioxazine Purple and paint tips. Use chisel edge and pull down lines in throat.

Use thinned down Hi-Lite Flesh and liner brush. Pull lines from outside in.

Use thinned Emperor's Gold. Pull lines from center out. Use stylus and put in center dots.

Helpful Hint:
When painting ribbon, lay your brush horizontally when shading and highlighting.

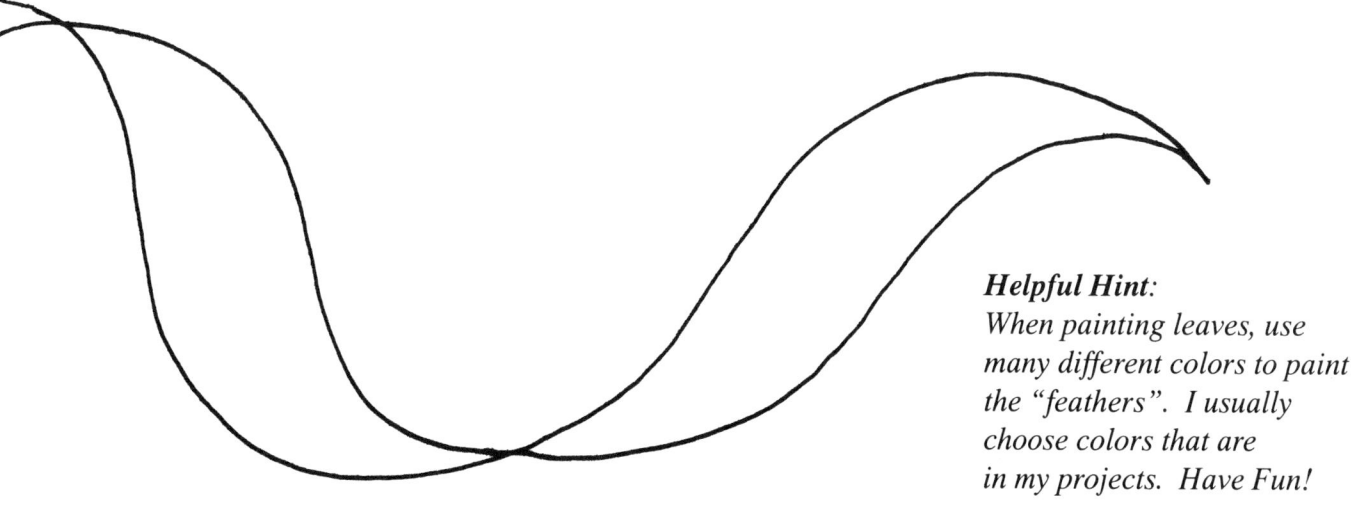

Morning Glory - Mailbox

Helpful Hint:
When painting leaves, use many different colors to paint the "feathers". I usually choose colors that are in my projects. Have Fun!

Morning Glory
Heart Wall Pocket

Palette - DecoArt Americana

Hi-Lite Flesh	Green Mist	Pansy Lavender	Titanium White
Mint Julep Green	Soft Lilac	Black/Green	Dioxazine Purple
Avocado	Brush'n Blend		

Brushes - Loew Cornell

#10 Flat	#2, #3 Round	#10/0 Liner	3/8" Angular Shader

Other Supplies

Graphite Paper Fine Block Sander
Tack Cloth Large Sponge Brush
Stylus Metal Heart Wall Pocket (Painter's Paradise)

Prep

Lightly sand and use tack cloth. Use the large sponge brush and basecoat the heart with **Mint Julep Green**. Let dry.

If you choose to use the patterns, now is the time to trace them on. Use the graphite paper and the stylus to trace pattern on the heart.

Morning Glories

Base both Morning Glories and the buds with **Soft Lilac** using either the flat brush or the angle brush. Let dry.

Use your angle brush with **Hi-Lite Flesh** on the tip and **Brush n' Blend** on the heel. Blend very well on your palette and paint the "smile" on your Morning Glories.

Purple Morning Glories - Refer to Morning Glories Worksheet

I used a flicking motion to achieve the thin lines in the Morning Glories. Use your #3 round, mix a little **Brush n' Blend** with **Pansy Lavendar** and "flick" all the way around the flower. (Tip: Flatten your round brush in the paint and blending gel. Start on the outside of your flower, start on chisel edge and "flick" toward the middle of the flower.)

Do this same technique with **Dioxazine Purple**. (Tip: "Flick" in various spots…not all the way around the flower.)

This is the fun part! Use an angle brush, dip the tip in **Dioxazine Purple** and **Brush n' Blend** on the heel. Blend well before painting on your surface. Laying the brush almost horizontally, make small strokes all the way around the Morning Glory following the shape of the flower.

Morning Glory - Heart Wall Pocket continued

At this point also shade on both sides of the neck of the flower. Use the chisel edge and pull in a few lines on the neck.

Use your liner and thinned down **Hi-Lite Flesh** and pull thin lines from the outside in (I usually pull these little lines in where the flower comes to a point).

Use thinned down **Emperor's Gold** and pull stamens from the inside out. Use your Stylus and put little dots in the smile.

Morning Glory Buds-Refer to Morning Glory Worksheet

Your buds are based in with Soft Lilac at this point. Use Dioxazine Purple on the tip and Brush n'Blend on the heel of your angle brush. Follow the pattern to put the lines in the buds.

Leaves - Refer to Leaf Worksheet

Base the leaves with **Avocado** and **Black Green**.

On this project I used **Mint Julep Green** to pull a vein from one end to the other end of the leaf with the chisel edge of my 3/8" angular brush. While the vein is wet, pull down some "feathers".

Use the same brush and pull in **Mint Julep Green** from the outside in and let dry.

Pull in **Pansy Lavender** from the outside in (just like you did with the **Mint Julep Green**).

Use your liner and mix **Titanium White** and **Mint Julep Green** together and add veins to your leaf.

Use your liner and pull from the outside in and only on one side with **Emperor's Gold**. I do not thin the paint when I paint these little accents on the leaf.

White Filler Flowers - Refer to Filler Flower Worksheet

I used a #2 round with **Titanium White**. I just touched and pulled in various spots.

Finishing

Let your piece dry completely and seal with J.W. Wipe-On Varnish. I use a damp cloth and varnish to seal my piece. *(Tip: Keep your damp used cloth in a ziplock bag. Use it over and over.)*

Decorative Rose Books
(Yard Sale Finds☺)

Palette - DecoArt Americana

Avocado	French Mauve	Emperor's Gold	Black Green
Cranberry Wine	Light Buttermilk	Mint Julep Green	Lemon Yellow
Antique Mauve	Evergreen	Burnt Umber	Olive Green
Brush'n Blend	Faux Glazing Medium		

Brushes - Loew Cornell

1/2" Angle Brush   #10/0 Liner   Old Flat Brush (for painting pages)

Other Brushes

3/4" Scheewe Foliage Angular S8037

Other Supplies

Graphite Paper   Sea Sponge
Stylus   Used Books (Yard Sale Finds)

Prep

To basecoat the book, use a sea sponge and pounce three colors. *(Tip: Soak the sponge until it becomes very soft...wrap and squeeze in a towel to get all the excess water out.)* Pounce in the **Mint Julep Green** first. Do the same procedure with the **Evergreen** and **Light Buttermilk**. Do not wash out the previous color. *(Tip: Do not over pounce! If your three colors look like one solid color after you are finished...you have pounced too much☹. Let dry and start again).*

Use **Emperor's Gold** and an old flat brush and paint the edge of the pages. This gives a finished look to the project. Let book dry completely.

If you choose to use the patterns, now is the time to trace them on. Use the graphite paper and the Stylus to trace pattern on the book.

Roses - Refer to Rose Worksheet

I have painted three colors of roses on this piece. I used **Cranberry Wine/Light Buttermilk, Antique Mauve/Light Buttermilk,** and **French Mauve /Light Buttermilk**.

Base in three rose shapes. **Cranberry Wine** (middle rose), **Antique Mauve** (bottom right) and **French Mauve** (top). Refer to the photograph for rose placement. Let dry.

Let's finish these roses☺...Using the 1/2" angular brush, dip the tip in **Light Buttermilk** and the heel of the brush in **Cranberry Wine** (or whatever base color rose you are working on). Blend and load until your brush is fully loaded....about 3/4th way up your bristles... *(Tip: I usually dip and blend at least four times before I'm ready to paint.)*

Use the Rose Worksheet as a guide. Start at the top...and while the top strokes are drying, skip down and do the sides and bottom. Come back and fill in the middle. All three roses are painted exactly the same way.

Decorative Rose Books continued

After these roses are completely dry, blend a little **Lemon Yellow** on the tip and glaze on the heel of the 1/2" angle brush. Stroke over a few of the lighter areas with **Lemon Yellow**.

Leaves - Refer to Leaf Worksheet

Base the leaves with **Avocado** and **Black Green**. I fit the leaves in and around the roses.

On this project I used **Olive Green** to pull a fine line from one end to the other end of the leaf with the chisel edge of my 1/2" angular brush. While the vein is wet, pull down some "feathers".

Use the same brush and pull in **Olive Green** from the outside in.

I pulled in some of the **French Mauve** from the outer part of the leaf toward the middle. *(Tip: I pull in all kinds of colors depending on the colors I used in my project. This is my favorite part of the painting a leaf ☺.)*

Use your liner and mix **Light Buttermilk** and **Olive Green** together and add veins to your leaf. *(Tip: Use plenty of water with your paint when pulling in veins.)*

Ribbon - Refer to Ribbon Worksheet

Mix one part **Mint Julep Green** with four parts of **Faux Glazing Medium**.
(Tip: The glaze will make the ribbon transparent, so adjust the color to your liking.) Use a 1/2" angular brush for the ribbon, but you can also get the same results by using a flat brush. Always start on chisel edge, press the bristles to the side, pull back up on chisel edge.

Shade the skinny parts of your ribbon with **Green Mist** on the tip and glaze in heel. Highlight the fat parts of your ribbon with **Light Buttermilk** in tip and glaze in heel. *(Tip: Use the **Green Mist** and **Light Buttermilk** sparingly and blend very well before shading and highlighting.*

Twigs - Refer to Twig Worksheet

I use watered down **Burnt Umber** and my liner brush to paint the little twigs. *(Tip: As you are painting the twigs, roll your brush between your fingers...it will make the twigs look a little more realistic.)*

Filler Flowers - Refer to Filler Flower Worksheet

Use the tip of the Foliage Brush and tap in **Light Buttermilk** where you feel the need.
(Tip: Let the brush sit in water for a couple of minutes before using. It will soften the bristles and make it easier to use.)

Finishing

Let your piece dry completely and seal with J.W. Wipe-On Varnish. I pour a little varnish on a damp cloth and gently rub over my piece. *(Tip: Store the damp cloth in a ziplock bag and use many, many times).*

Shabby Chic White Tray

Palette - DecoArt Americana
    Soft Lilac   Green Mist   Titanium White   Black Green
    Cadmium Yellow   Avocado   Emperor's Gold   Deep Periwinkle
    Lemon Yellow   Blend n' Brush   Faux Glazing Medium

Brushes - Loew Cornell
    5/8" Angular   #10/0 Liner   #3 Filbert
    Old Scruffy Brush for stenciling background

Other Supplies
    Fine Sanding Block and Tack Cloth   J.W. Wipe On Varnish
    Graphite Paper   Stylus
    Distressed White Tray   Delta Stencil Magic - Chintz #958611013

Prep

This tray was already painted white. Use a fine sanding block and sanded some of the paint off to give it a shabby chic look. After sanding, use a tack cloth to remove all dust

Background Stencil

This stencil fits perfectly on the inside of this tray. Use an old scruffy brush and tap in **Soft Lilac**. *(Tip: Use very little paint for this process.)* Let dry.

Roses - Refer to Rose Worksheet

These roses were painted with a 5/8" angular brush. Basecoat these with **Deep Periwinkle** and let dry. With **Titanium White** on the tip and **Deep Periwinkle** on the heel paint all three roses the same.

After these roses are dry, use your 5/8" angular brush with **Lemon Yellow** on the tip and glaze on the heel. Highlight a few of the petals.

Use **Emperor's Gold** and your Stylus to paint in the little dots in the middle of the roses.

Ribbons - Refer to Ribbon Worksheet

Mix one part **Soft Lilac** with four parts of Faux Glazing Medium. *(Tip: The glaze will make the ribbon transparent, so adjust the color to your liking.)* Use a 5/8" angular brush for ribbon, but you can also get the same results by using a flat brush. Always start on chisel edge, press the bristles to the side, pull back up on chisel edge. Refer to worksheet.

I used my liner brush and thinned down **Titanium White** and painted little lines across the ribbon (these ribbons would look good with or without the lines). Shade with **Deep Periwinkle** and highlight with **Titanium White**.

Shabby Chic White Tray continued
Leaves - Refer to Leaf Worksheet

Use the 5/8" angular brush and base the leaves with **Avocado** and **Black Green**. Let dry.

Using the same brush, pull a vein from one end to the other end of the leaf with the chisel edge. While the vein is wet, pull down some "feathers" with **Green Mist**. Highlight on the opposite side with **Green Mist**, let dry. After leaf is dry, pull through some **Soft Lilac**.

Use your liner and mix **Titanium White** and **Green Mist** with water. Add the veins to the leaf.

Use your liner and pull from outside in and only on one side with **Emperor's Gold**. I do not thin the paint when I paint these little accents on the leaves.

Filler Flowers - Refer to Filler Flower Worksheet

Use the #3 Filbert and **Titanium White** and press and pull some little filler flowers here and there. Use your stylus and **Cadmium Yellow** to put small little dots in the centers.

Finishing

Let your piece completely dry and seal with J.W. Wipe-On Varnish. I use a damp cloth and varnish to seal my piece.

ATTACH PATTERN HERE

Rose

Use angle brush and basecoat.

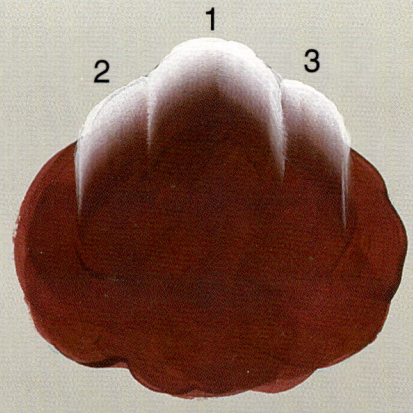
Use angle brush. White on tip and Cranberry Wine on heel. Start with center and work out to the sides.

The second and third steps are full strokes from one end to the other.

After putting the bud in place, take the strokes from each side and pull in front.

While letting the top portion dry, pat in the sides and bottom.

Fill in the middle of the rose with comma strokes. Gold dots in middle.

Leaf Worksheet

Base coat fully with Avocado. Base top portion with Black Green.

Using an angle brush make curved line with Mint Julep Green. Pull feathers from curved line.

Using same angle brush, pull Mint Julep Green from the outside in.

Pull in French Mauve from the outside in.

Use liner brush and pull through vines.

Use liner brush and pull Gold accent lines in.

Rose Votive Candle Holders

Palette - DecoArt Americana

Avocado	Fleshtone	Black Green	Silver Sage Green
Heritage Brick	Green Mist	Emperor's Gold	Light Buttermilk
Titanium White	Blend n' Brush	Faux Glazing Medium	

Brushes - Loew Cornell

3/8", 1/4" Angular   #10 Flat   #10/0 Liner

Other Brushes

1/4" Scheewe Foliage Angular S8035

Other Supplies

J.W. Etc. White Lightning   Fine Sanding Block and Tack Cloth
Large Sponge Brush   J.W. Wipe-On Varnish
Graphite Paper   Stylus
Wooden Votive Holders (set of 3 - Artist's Club)

Prep

Lightly sand wooden votive candle holders until smooth to the touch. Wipe with tack cloth to remove any dust. Mix J.W. White Lightning and **Silver Sage Green**. Use the large sponge brush and basecoat the votive holders. *(Tip: I use equal parts of paint and White Lightning.)* Lightly sand again, and base one more time if desired. Let dry.

Top Rims

Paint the top of each candle with **Black Green** (I used two coats and my #10 flat brush)...let dry. Use the small foliage brush and lightly tap **Emperor's Gold**.

Roses - Refer to Rose Worksheet

Use a 3/8" angular shader and base the roses with **Heritage Brick**. Use **Light Buttermilk** on the tip and **Heritage Brick** on the heel.

Leaves - Refer to Leaf Worksheet

Base leaves with **Avocado** and **Black Green** using a 1/2" angular shader. Let dry.

Follow Leaf Worksheet to build the rest of the leaf. Use **Mint Julep Green** for the "feathers" on each side the leaves. Use **Mint Julep Green**, **Titanium White** and water for the veins. Pull in **Emperor's Gold** on one side of the leaf.

Ribbon - Refer to Ribbon Worksheet

Mix one part **Green Mist** with four parts of Faux Glazing Medium. Use the 3/8" angular brush. Always start on chisel edge, press the bristles to the side, pull back up on chisel edge.

Rose Votive Candle Holder continued

Shade the skinny parts of your ribbon with **Green Mist** on tip and glaze in heel.
Highlight the fat parts of your ribbon with **Titanium White** in tip and glaze in heel.

Little White Highlights

Use **Titanium White** and the small foliage brush and tap in a little white here and there.

Finishing

Let your piece completely dry and seal with J.W. Wipe-On Varnish. I use a damp cloth and varnish to seal my piece.

Enjoy painting this piece!!

Rose Votive Candle Holders

Wild Rose Blossoms - Votive Candle Holders

Palette - DecoArt Americana
Avocado	Antique Mauve	Emperor's Gold	Black Green
Titanium White	Brush n' Blend	Hi-Lite Flesh	Cadmium Yellow
Burnt Umber	Mint Julep Green	Bosenberry Pink	
Faux Glazing Medium			

Brushes - Loew Cornell
3/8" Angular	#10/0 Liner	#6, #10 Flat	#2 Round

Other Brushes
1/4" Scheewe Foliage Angular S8035

Other Supplies
J.W. Etc. White Lightning
Large Sponge Brush
Graphite Paper (Gray and White)
Cotton Swabs
Wooden Votive Holders (set of 3 - Artist's Club)
Fine Sanding Block and Tack Cloth
J. W. Wipe-On Varnish
Stylus

Prep
Lightly sand wooden votive candle holders until smooth to the touch. Mix J.W. White Lightning and **Silver Sage Green**. Use the large sponge brush and basecoat the votive holders. (Tip: I use equal parts of paint and White Lightening). Lightly sand again, and base one more time if desired. Let dry.

Top Rims
Paint the top of each candle with **Black Green** (I used two coats and my #10 flat brush)...let dry. Use the small foliage brush and lightly tap **Emperor's Gold**.

Wild Rose Blossoms - Refer to Wild Rose Blossom Worksheet
Use your #6 flat and base in all the blossoms with **Hi-Lite Flesh**. Let dry.

I randomly use both **Antique Mauve** and **Bosenberry Pink**. Paint all around the blossoms using these two colors. Color is on the tip of your 3/8" angular brush and Brush n' Blend on the heel. Let dry.

Use your liner and thinned down **Titanium White**, pull little white lines from the inside out. Do this on each petal.

Use your #2 round brush and **Cadmium Yellow** and dab a little yellow in the middle of each blossom. Let dry. Use your stylus and paint small dots with **Black Green**.

Use your #2 round and paint the white highlights on the tips of the petals. Use **TitaniumWhite** and fully load your brush. Start on chisel edge, press, and then come back up on chisel edge. (*Tip: I don't paint these on every petal.*)

Wild Rose Blossoms - Votive Candle Holders continued
Leaves - Refer to Leaf Worksheet
Base the leaves with **Avocado** and **Black Green**.

Use **Mint Julep Green** to pull a vein from one end to the other end of the leaf with the chisel edge of my 3/8" angular brush. While the vein is wet, pull in some "feathers".

Use the same brush and pull **Mint Julep Green** from the outside in and let dry.

I pulled in some of the **French Mauve**. Pull in just like you did the **Mint Julep Green**. *(Tip: I pull in all kinds of colors depending on the colors I used in my project. This is my favorite part of painting a leaf.)* ☺

Use your liner and mix **Titanium White** and **Mint Julep Green** together and add veins to your leaf.

Use your liner and pull from the outside in and only on one side the **Emperor's Gold**. Do not thin the paint when I paint these little accents on the leaf.

Filler Berries - Refer to Berry Worksheet
I always have a pencil with an unused eraser or cotton swabs. Use the end of the eraser or the cotton swabs to make these little berries. *(Tip: I use these little berries instead of filler flowers on a lot of projects.)* Dip into a little **Faux Glaze Medium** first, then dip into **Mint Julep Green** on one side and Emperor's Gold on the other. *(Tip: Pounce a couple times before putting directly on your surface.)* Use your liner and thinned down **Titanium White** and put little dots in each berry.

Outlined Blossoms
Use the liner brush and watered down **Emperor's Gold** and roughly outline the blossoms and leaves.

Twigs - Refer to Twig Worksheet
I use watered down **Burnt Umber** and my liner brush to paint the little twigs. *(Tip: As you are painting the twigs, roll your brush between your fingers....it will make the twigs look a little more realistic.)*

Finishing
Let your piece completely dry and seal with J.W. Wipe-On Varnish. Use a damp cloth and varnish to seal the piece. ☺

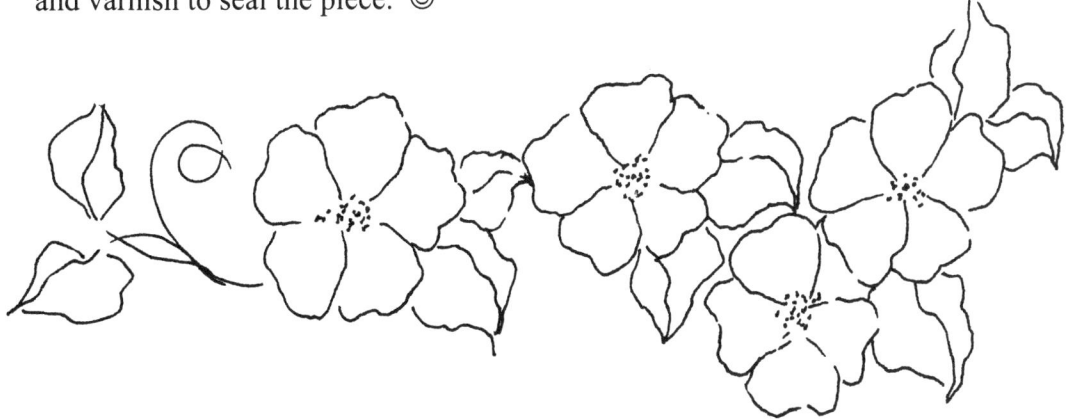

Wild Rose Blossoms
Votive Candle Holders

Wild Rose Blossoms
Metal Wall Pocket

Wild Rose Blossoms - Metal Wall Pocket

Palette - DecoArt Americana
- Avocado
- Titanium White
- Burnt Umber
- Brush n' Blend
- French Mauve
- Antique Mauve
- Mint Julep Green
- Faux Glazing Medium
- Emperor's Gold
- Hi-Lite Flesh
- Bosenberry Pink
- Black Green
- Cadmium Yellow
- Payne's Gray

Brushes - Loew Cornell
- 3/8" Angular
- #10, #12, #3 Flat
- #10/0 Liner
- #2 Round

Other Supplies
- Tack Cloth
- Graphite Paper
- Metal Wall Pocket (Michael's Craft Store)
- J. W. Wipe on Varnish
- Stylus

Prep

Wipe metal wall pocket with tack cloth. If you choose to use the patterns, trace them on at this point with graphite paper. Do not trace all the small detail.

Wild Rose Blossoms - Refer to Wild Rose Blossom Worksheet

Use your #3 flat and base in all the blossoms with **Hi-Lite Flesh**. Let dry.

Use your 3/8" angular brush to paint in the shading. Randomly use **Antique Mauve** and **Bosenberry Pink** on the tip of your 3/8" angular brush and use Brush n' Blend on the heel of the brush. Paint all around the blossoms using these two colors. Let dry.

Use your liner and thinned down **Titanium White**, pull little white lines from the inside out. Do this on each petal.

Use your #2 brush and **Cadmium Yellow** and dab a little yellow in the middle of each blossom. Let dry. Use your Stylus and put small dots with **Payne's Gray**.

Use your #2 round and paint the white highlights on the tips of the petals. Use **Titanium White** and fully load your brush. Start on chisel edge, press, and then come back up on chisel edge.

Leaves - Refer to Leaf Worksheet

Base the leaves with **Avocado** and **Black Green**.

Use **Mint Julep Green** to pull a vein from one end to the other end of the leaf with the chisel edge of my 3/8" angular brush. While the vein is wet, pull down some "feathers".

Use the same brush and pull in **Mint Julep Green** from the outside of the leaf toward the middle and let dry.

Wild Rose Blossoms continued
Pull in some of the **French Mauve**. Pull in just like you did the **Mint Julep Green**.

Use your liner and mix **Titanium White** and **Mint Julep Green** together and add veins to your leaf. (*Tip: Be sure to thin down paint mixture before painting veins.*)

Use your liner and pull from the outside in and only on one side the **Emperor's Gold**.

Shadow Leaves - Refer to Shadow Leaf Worksheet
Use the #10 or #12 flat brush to make these shadow leaves. Mix **Avocado** with **Emperor's Gold**. (Tip: Use more **Emperor's Gold** than **Avocado**.) Mix in a couple of drops of Faux Glazing Medium and paint the shadow leaves.

Twigs/Branch - Refer to Twigs/Branch Worksheet
I use watered down **Burnt Umber** and my liner brush to paint the little twigs.

Finishing
Let your piece completely dry and seal with J.W. Wipe-On Varnish. I use a damp cloth and varnish to seal my piece.

Wild Rose Blossoms - Crackled Clock

Palette - DecoArt Americana
Avocado	French Mauve	Emperor's Gold	Black Green
Titanium White	Antique Mauve	Hi-Lite Flesh	Cadmium Yellow
Burnt Umber	Mint Julep Green	Bosenberry Pink	Winter Blue
French Grey Blue	Brush n' Blend	Faux Glazing Medium	

Brushes - Loew Cornell
3/8", 5/8" Angular   #10/0 Liner   #12, #6 Flat   #2 Round

Other Supplies
Tack Cloth   J. W. Wipe-On Varnish
Graphite Paper   Stylus
Crackled Clock (Artist's Club)

Morning Glory Mailbox

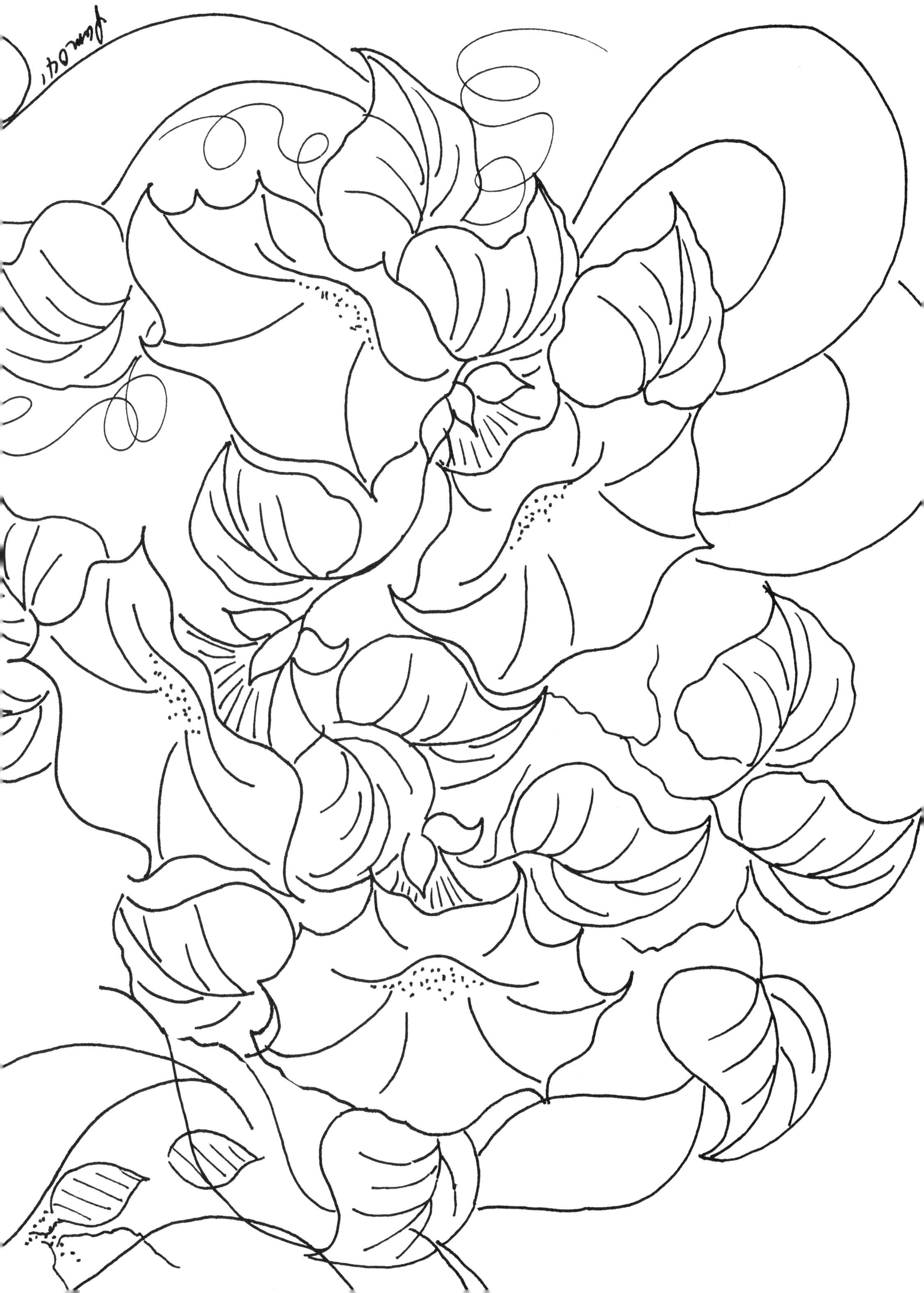

Wild Rose Blossoms
(*Black Chalkboard*)

Morning Glory
Thermometer

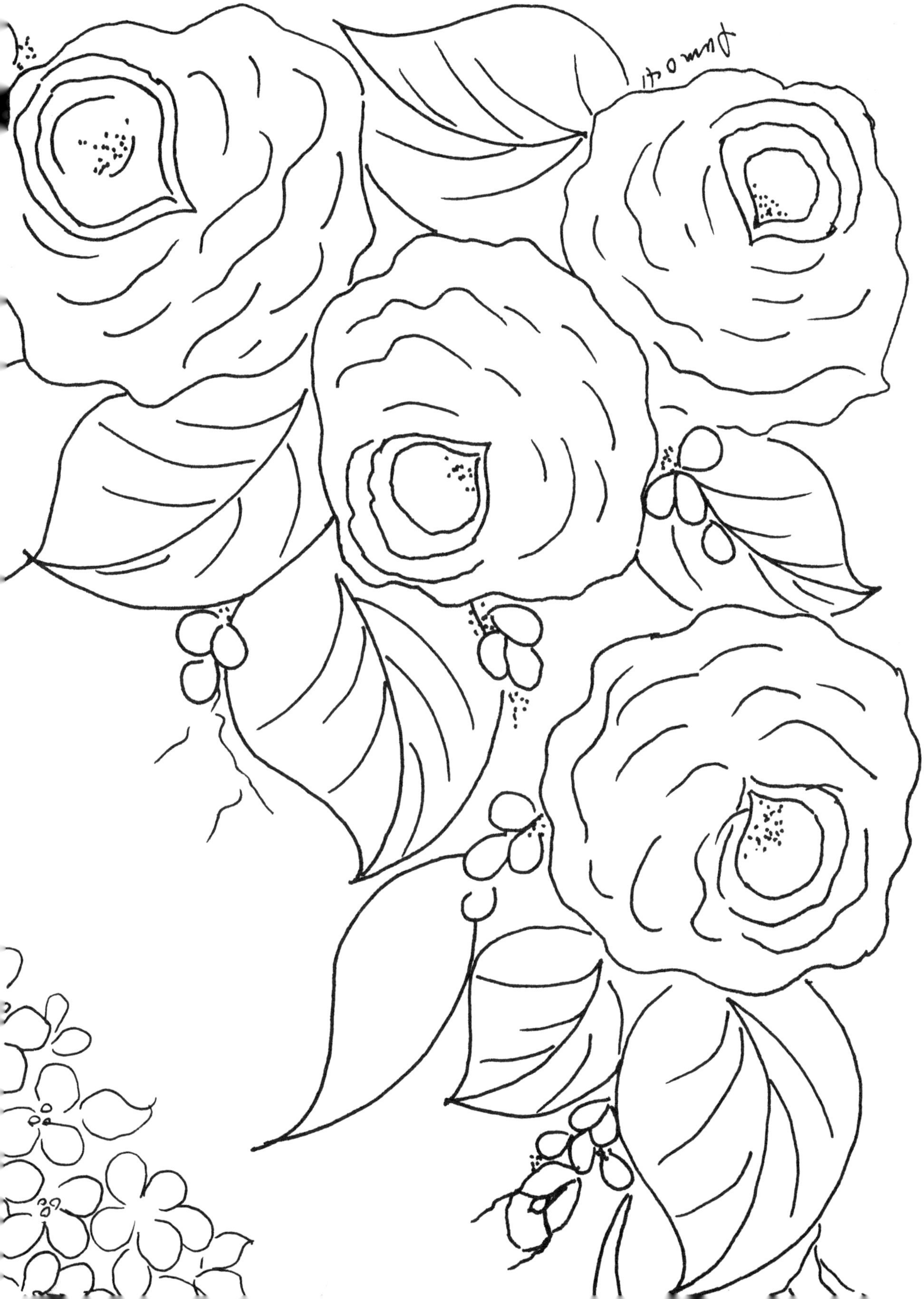

Decorative Rose Lamp

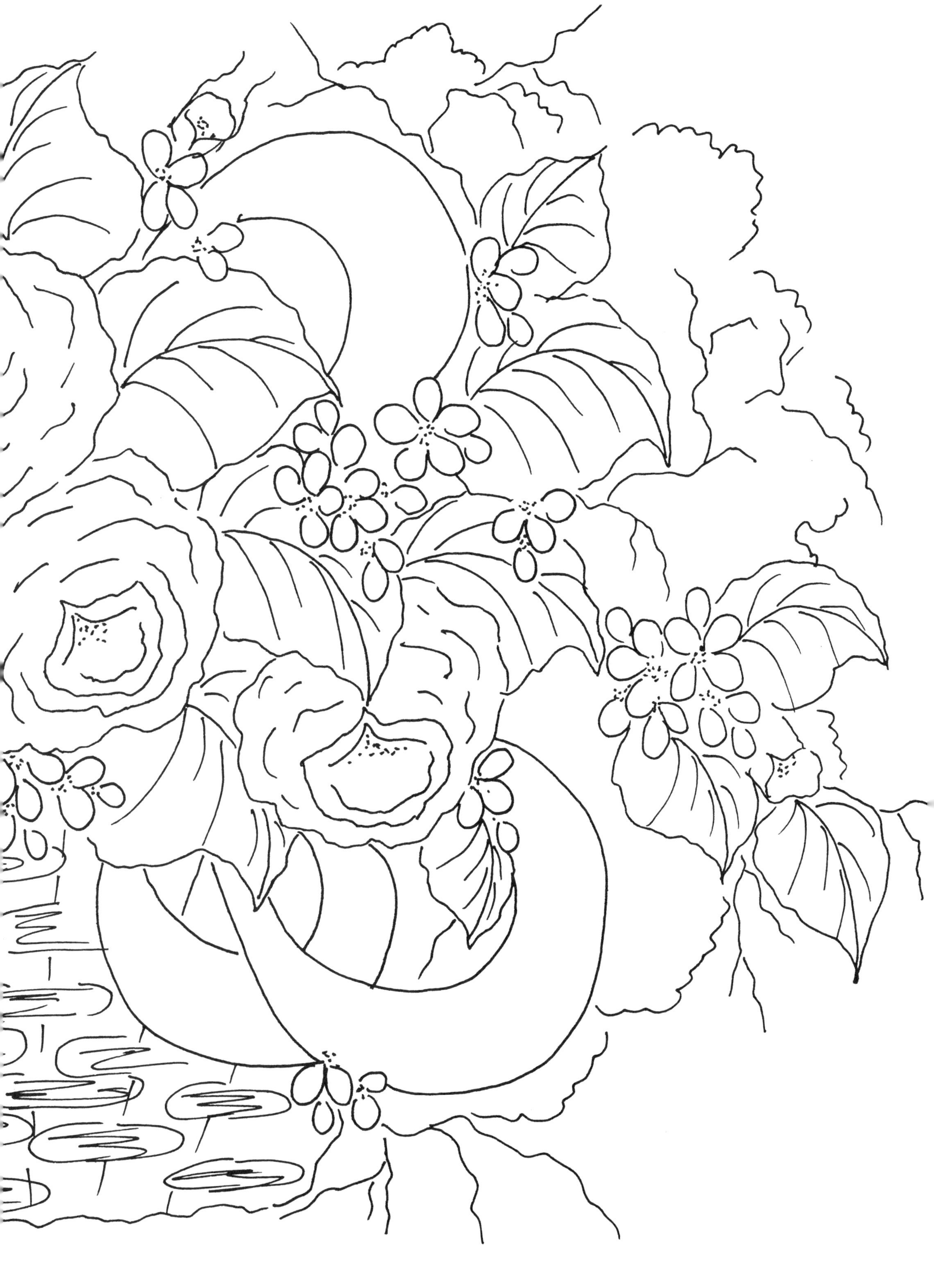

Chalk It Up With Roses
(Black Chalkboard)

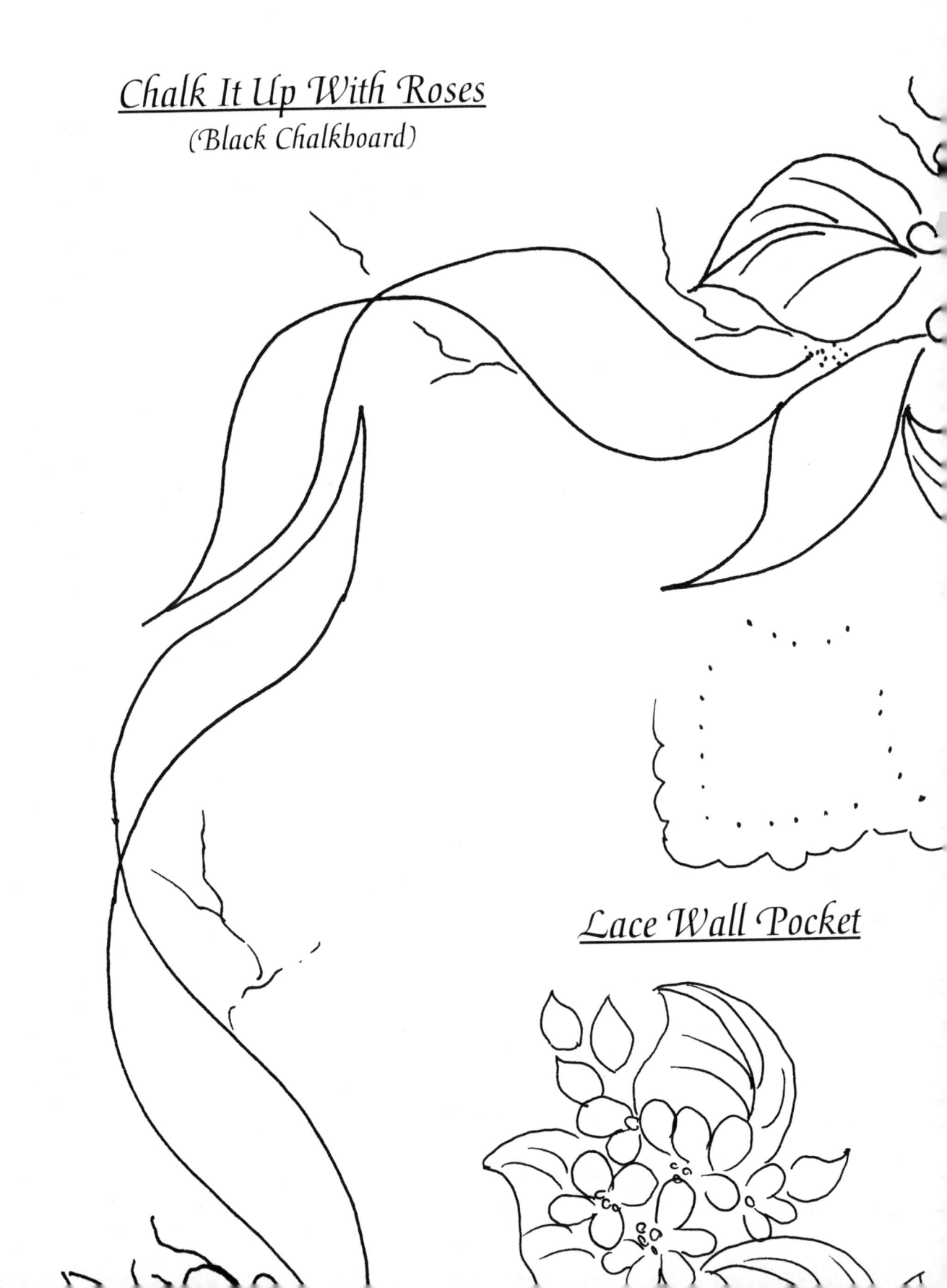

Lace Wall Pocket

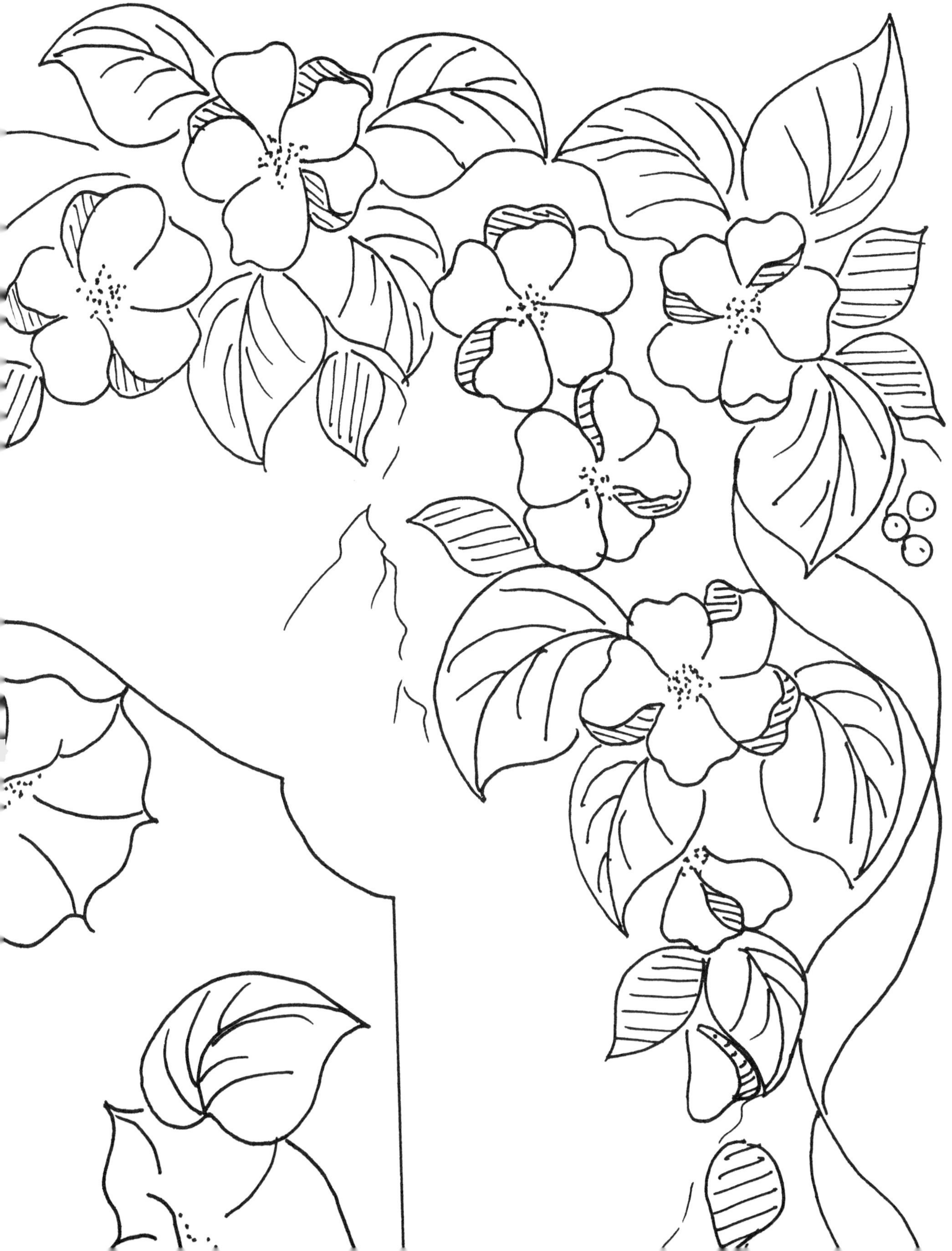

Large Rose Clock

Wild Rose Blossoms continued
Prep
There is no prep on this piece. It comes crackled and ready to paint!

If you choose to use the patterns, trace them on at this point with graphite paper. Do not trace all the small detail.

Blossoms - Refer to Wild Rose Blossom Worksheet
Use your #6 flat and base in all the blossoms with **Hi-Lite Flesh**. Let dry.

Use your 3/8" angular brush to paint in the shading. Randomly use **Antique Mauve** and **Bosenberry Pink** on the tip of your 3/8" angular brush and use Brush n' Blend on the heel of the brush. Let dry.

Use your liner and thinned down **Titanium White**, pull little white lines from the inside out. Do this on each petal.

Use your #2 brush and **Cadmium Yellow** and dab a little yellow in the middle of each blossom. Let dry. Use your Stylus and put small dots with **Black Green**.

Use your #2 round and paint the white highlights on the tips of the petals. Use **Titanium White** and fully load your brush. Start on chisel edge, press, and then come back up on chisel edge. (*Tip: I don't paint these on every petal.*)

Leaves - Refer to Leaf Worksheet
Base the leaves with **Avocado** and **Black Green**.

Use **Mint Julep Green** to pull a vein from one end to the other end of the leaf with the chisel edge of my 3/8" angular brush. While the vein is wet, pull down some "feathers".

Use the same brush and pull in **Mint Julep Green** from the outside in and let dry.

This is the fun part! I pulled in some of the **French Mauve**. Pull in just like you did the **Mint Julep Green**.

Use your liner and mix **Titanium White** and **Mint Julep Green** together and add veins to your leaf.

Use your liner and pull from the outside in and only on one side the **Emperor's Gold**. I do not thin the paint when I paint these little accents on the leaf.

Ribbon - Refer to Ribbon Worksheet
Use your 5/8" angular brush for the ribbon. I mixed one part **Winter Blue** with four parts of Faux Glazing Medium. Always start on chisel edge, press the bristles to the side, pull back up on chisel edge.

Wild Rose Blossoms - Ribbon continued

Shade the skinny parts of your ribbon with **French Grey Blue** on tip and glaze in heel. Highlight the fat parts of your ribbon with **Titanium White** in tip and glaze in heel.

(Tip: Use the **Titanium White** and **French Grey Blue** sparingly and blend very well before shading/highlighting.)

Filler Berries - Refer to Berry Worksheet

I always have a pencil with an unused eraser or cheap Qtips on my table. Use the end of the eraser or the Qtips to make these little berries. *(Tip: I use these little berries instead of filler flowers on a lot of projects.)* Dip into a little **Faux Glaze Medium** first, then dip into **French Mauve** and a little **Emperor's Gold**. Use your liner and dab a little **Titanium White** on each berry as highlights.

Twigs - Refer to Twig Worksheet

I use watered down **Burnt Umber** and my liner brush to paint the little twigs.

Finishing

Let your piece completely dry and seal with J.W. Wipe-On Varnish. I use a damp cloth and varnish to seal my piece.

Painting Tip:

When I use Faux Glazing Medium, I pour a small amount into a SOLO 202 cup. (These are used for condiments.) Never mix glazing medium with water. The two work against each other.

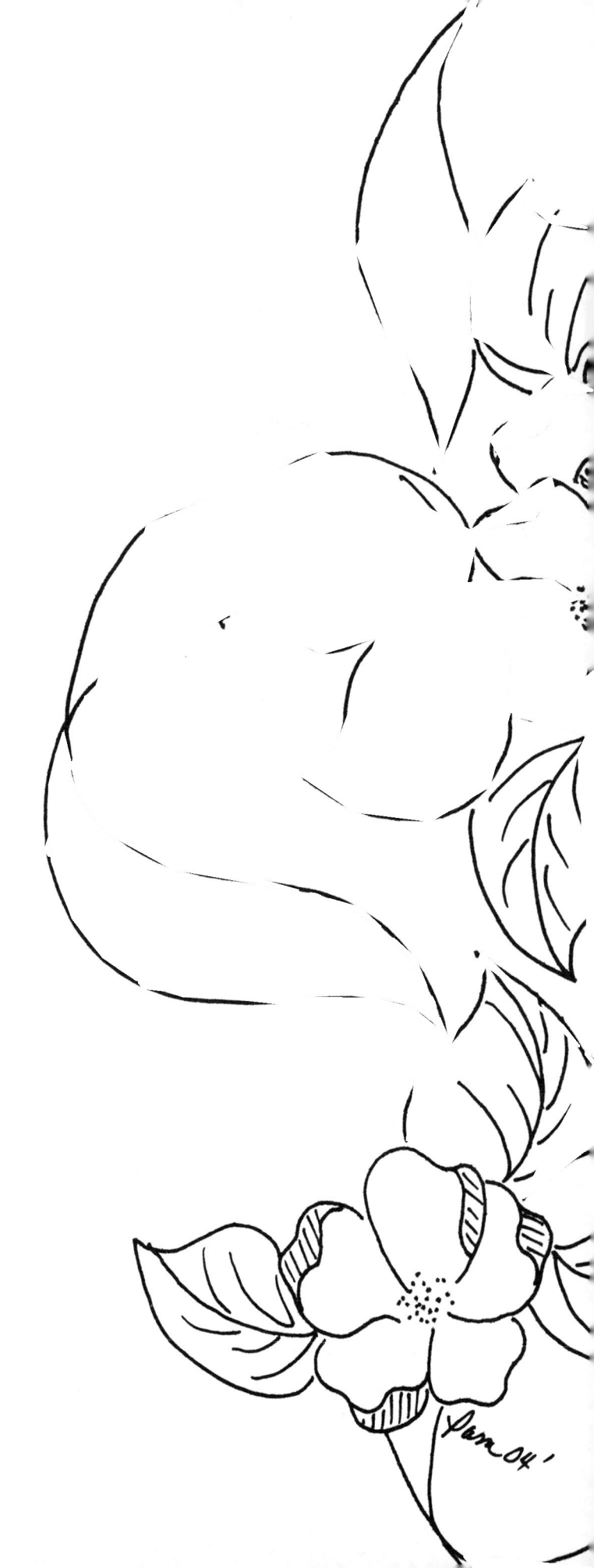

Wild Rose Blossoms
Crackled Clock

Shabby Chic White Mirror

Palette - DecoArt Americana

Soft Lilac	Green Mist	Titanium White	Black Green
Wisteria	Avocado	Emperor's Gold	Deep Periwinkle
Olive Green	Blend n' Brush	Faux Glazing Medium	

Brushes - Loew Cornell

1/2" Angular   #10/0 Liner   #3 Filbert
Old Scruffy Brush for stenciling background

Shabby Chic White Mirror

Other Supplies

Fine Sanding Block and Tack Cloth
Graphite Paper
Stylus
Delta Stencil Magic - Chintz #958611013
J.W. Wipe On Varnish
Tape
Distressed White Mirror

Prep

Base this wooden mirror with **Titanium White**. Let dry completely. Use the sanding block and "rough up" some of the edges. Use the tack cloth to remove any dust. I only put one coat of paint on this mirror.

Background Stencil

Tape stencil on top of the wooden part of this piece. Use an old scruffy brush and tap in **Deep Periwinkle**. *(Tip: Use very little paint for this process.)* Let dry.

Roses - Refer to Rose Worksheet

These roses were painted with a 1/2" angular brush. Basecoat one rose with **Wisteria** and the other two with **Deep Periwinkle**. Let dry. With **Titanium White** on the tip and **Deep Periwinkle** on the heel, paint two of the roses. With **Titanium White** on the tip and **Wisteria** on the heel, paint one rose.

Refer to Rose Worksheet for painting the rose buds.

Use **Emperor's Gold** and your Stylus to paint in the little dots in the middle of the roses.

Ribbons - Refer to Ribbon Worksheet

Mix one part **Soft Lilac** with four parts of Faux Glazing Medium. Use a 1/2" angular brush for ribbon, but you can also get the same results by using a flat brush. Always start on chisel edge, press the bristles to the side, pull back up on chisel edge.

Shade with **Deep Periwinkle** and highlight with **Titanium White**.

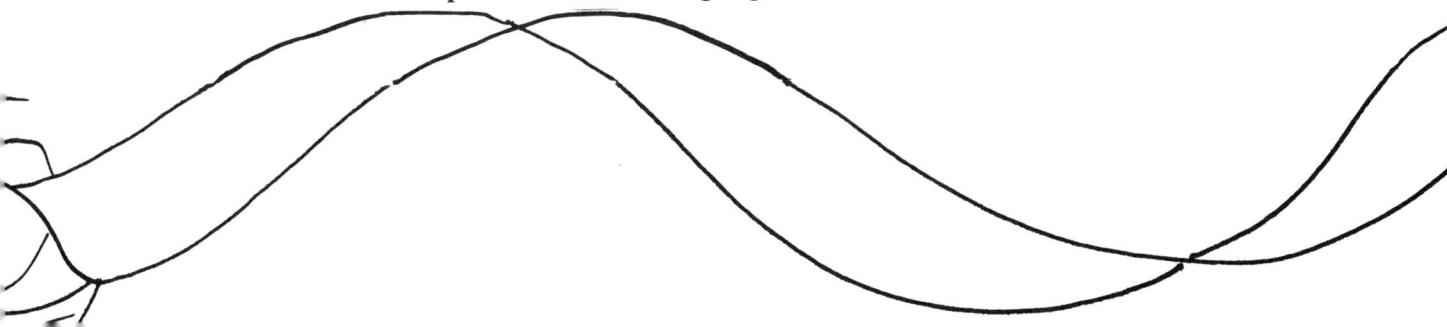

Shabby Chic White Mirror continued

Leaves - Refer to Leaf Worksheet

Base leaves with the 1/2" angular brush. Use **Avocado** and **Black Green**. Let dry.

Use the 1/2" angular on the leaves. Using **Green Mist**, pull a vein from one end to the other end of the leaf with the chisel edge. While the vein is wet, pull down some "feathers" with **Green Mist**. Highlight on the opposite side with **Green Mist**, let dry. After leaf is dry, pull through some **Soft Lilac**.

Use your liner and mix **Titanium White** and **Green Mist** with water. Add the veins to the leaf.

Use your liner and pull from outside in and only on one side with **Emperor's Gold**. I do not thin the paint when I paint these little accents on the leaves.

Cluster Flowers - Refer to Filler Flower Worksheet

These cluster flowers are just groupings of my filler flowers. I used a #3 filbert brush and **Olive Green** and **Titanium White** to paint these flowers. I paint three or four little petals together...alternating with the two colors and sometimes mixing them together. Use your Stylus and **Titanium White** and **Black Green** to put small little dots in the centers.

Finishing

Let your piece completely dry and seal with J.W. Wipe-On Varnish. I use a damp cloth and varnish to seal my piece.

Tissue Box

Palette - DecoArt Americana

Soft Lilac	Green Mist	Titanium White	Black Green
Grape Juice	Cadmium Yellow	Avocado	Emperor's Gold
Deep Periwinkle	Blend n' Brush	Faux Glazing Medium	

Brushes - Loew Cornell

1/2" Angular   #10/0 Liner   #3 Filbert
Old Scruffy Brush for stenciling lace

Other Supplies

Fine Sanding Block and Tack Cloth   Large Sponge Brush
J.W. Wipe On Varnish   Graphite Paper
Scissors   Tape
Wilton Paper Doilies 10x14   Stylus
Wooden Tissue Box (Woodcrafts)

Tissue Box continued
Prep
Lightly sand wooden tissue box until smooth to the touch. Use the large sponge brush and basecoat the box with **Soft Lilac**. Let dry. Lightly sand again, and base one more time if desired. Let dry.

Lace
Use doilies to achieve the look of lace on this piece. I cut and used the corners of the paper doilies. Hold in place with tape and use scruffy brush and **Titanium White** to lightly pounce on the lace look. *(Tip: Use very little paint for this process.)* Continue to pounce the lace design around the box. Use the pattern for placement.

Use the 1/2" angular brush to paint the shading around the lace. Use **Deep Periwinkle** on the tip and Glaze on the heel. Lay the brush down horizontally and pull the shading around the lace.

You can use your liner and thinned down **Titanium White** to reinforce some of the lines around the outside of the lace.

Roses - Refer to Rose Worksheet
Refer to the worksheet for shape of the roses. I used **Grape Juice** as the base color for these roses. I used a 1/2" angular brush with **Titanium White** on the tip and **Grape Juice** on the heel. *(Tip: If your brush starts to drag...dip in a small amount of Brush n' Blend, blend and paint again.)*

Buds - Refer to Rose Worksheet
Use **Grape Juice** and **Titanium White** to paint these rose buds.
Use the stylus and **Emperor's Gold** and put the little dots in the center of the roses and buds.

Leaves - Refer to Leaf Worksheet
Base leaves with the 1/2" angular brush. I used **Avocado** and **Black Green**. Let dry.

Use the 1/2" angular on the leaves. Use **Green Mist** and pull a vein from one end to the other end of the leaf with the chisel edge. While the vein is wet, pull down some "feathers" with **Green Mist**. Highlight on the opposite side with **Green Mist**, let dry. After leaf is dry, pull through some **Soft Lilac**.

Use your liner brush, thin down **Titanium White** and **Green Mist**. Add the veins to the leaf.

Use your liner and pull from the outside in and only on one side the **Emperor's Gold**. I do not thin the paint when I paint these little accents on the leaves.

White Filler Flowers - Refer to Filler Flower Worksheet
Use the #3 Filbert and **Titanium White** and press and pull some little filler flowers here and there. Use your Stylus and **Cadmium Yellow** to put small little dots in the centers.

Finishing
Let your piece completely dry and seal with J.W. Wipe-On Varnish. I use a damp cloth and varnish to seal my piece.

Tissue Box

BASKET OF ROSES MAILBOX PAGES 46 - 49 PULLOUT

BASKET OF
ROSES MAILBOX
PAGES 46 - 49
PULLOUT

End

Wooden Rose Frame

Palette - DecoArt Americana
- Avocado
- Black Green
- Light Buttermilk
- Faux Glazing Medium
- Mauve
- Cadmium Yellow
- Blend n' Brush
- Burnt Umber
- Heritage Brick
- Titanium White
- French Mauve
- Emperor's Gold
- Mint Julep Green

Brushes - Loew Cornell
1/2", 5/8" Angular   #10, 1" Flat   #10/0 Liner   #2 Round

Other Supplies
- Fine Sanding Block and Tack Cloth
- J.W. Wipe On Varnish
- Stylus
- Large Brush (base coating)
- Graphite Paper
- Wooden Frame (Michaels Craft Store)

Prep
Lightly sand wooden frame until smooth to the touch. Use the 1" flat brush and base the entire frame with **Light Buttermilk**. After completely dry, wet a small area with Brush n' Blend. Use the 1" flat brush and pick up a small amount of **Mint Julep Green** and slip-slap over the wet area with a very light touch. *(Tip: Be sure to let some of the lighter color show through.)* Continue to wet and slip-slap the entire frame. Let dry completely and lightly sand. Cover the edge of the frame completely with **Mint Julep Green**.

Roses - Refer to Rose Worksheet
Use a 1/2" angular shader and base the roses with **Heritage Brick**. Use **Light Buttermilk** on the tip and **Heritage Brick** on the heel.

Use **Cadmium Yellow** and your stylus to make the small dots in the buds and roses.

Leaves - Refer to Leaf Worksheet
Base leaves with **Avocado** and **Black Green** using a 1/2" angular shader. Let dry.

Follow Leaf Worksheet to build the rest of the leaf. Use **Mint Julep Green** for the "feathers". Use **French Mauve** on the opposite side and pull toward the middle. Use **Mint Julep Green**, **Titanium White** and water for the veins. Pull in **Emperor's Gold** on one side of the leaf.

Ribbon - Refer to Ribbon Worksheet
Mix one part **French Mauve** with four parts of Faux Glazing Medium. Use the 1/2" angular brush. Always start on chisel edge, press the bristles to the side, pull back up on chisel edge.

Shade the skinny parts of your ribbon with **Mauve** on tip and glaze in heel. Highlight the fat parts of your ribbon with **Titanium White** in tip and glaze in heel.

Wooden Rose Frame continued
Little White Highlights - Refer to Worksheet
Use **Light Buttermilk** and pull in little filler flowers here and there.

Twigs - Refer to Worksheet
Use thinned down **Burnt Umber** and your liner brush to paint the twigs. *(Tip: Roll the brush between your fingers to make a more natural looking twig.)*

Shadow Leaves - Refer to Worksheet
Mix Faux Glazing Medium and a small amount of **Emperor's Gold** to make the stroke leaves. I used the #10 flat brush.

Finishing
Let your piece completely dry and seal with J.W. Wipe-On Varnish. I use a damp cloth and varnish to seal my piece.

Enjoy painting this piece!!

Large Rose Clock

Palette - DecoArt Americana

Shading Flesh	Avocado	Dark Chocolate	Fleshtone
Black Green	Silver Sage Green	Heritage Brick	Green Mist
Emperor's Gold	Light Buttermilk	Titanium White	Blend n' Brush
Faux Glazing Medium			

Brushes - Loew Cornell

5/8", 1/2" Angular   #10 Flat   #10/0 Liner

Other Supplies

J.W. Etc. White Lightning   Fine Sanding Block and Tack Cloth
Large Sponge Brush   J.W. Wipe On Varnish
Graphite Paper   Stylus
Large Wooden Clock (Artist's Club)

Prep

Lightly sand wooden clock until smooth to the touch. Mix **J.W. White Lightning** and **Silver Sage Green** together. Use the large sponge brush and basecoat the clock. *(Tip: I use equal parts of paint and White Lightening.)* Lightly sand again, and base one more time if desired. Let dry and then let's paint.

Roses

I have mixed two colors together and basecoated these roses. Put the darker color (**Heritage Brick**) at the top and then put the lighter color (**Shading Flesh**) on the bottom.

Base in the shape of the rose using the above colors. *See Rose Worksheet*. Build the rose using **Light Buttermilk** on the tip and **Heritage Brick** and **Shading Flesh** on the heel. Use the Rose Worksheet as a guide to build the roses. *(Tip: If your brush starts to drag…dip in a small amount of Brush n' Blend, blend and paint again.)*

Leaves - Refer to Leaf Worksheet

Base leaves with **Avocado** and **Black Green**. Let dry.

Use the 1/2" angular on the leaves. Pull a vein from one end to the the other end of the leaf with the chisel edge. While the vein is wet, pull down some "feathers" with **Green Mist**. Highlight on the opposite side with **Green Mist**, let dry, and then with **Fleshtone**.

Use your liner and mix **Light Buttermilk**, **Green Mist** and water together. Add the veins to the leaf.

Use your liner and pull from the outside in and only on one side the **Emperor's Gold**. I do not thin the paint when I paint these little accents on the leaf.

Large Rose Clock continued

Shadow Leaves - Refer to Shadow Leaves Worksheet

Use the #10 flat brush to make these shadow leaves. Mix **Avocado** with **Emperor's Gold** (Tip: Use more **Emperor's Gold** than **Avocado**. Mix in a couple of drops of **Faux Glazing Medium** and paint the leaves.

Ribbon - Refer to Ribbon Worksheet

Mix one part **Green Mist** with four parts of **Faux Glazing Medium**. Use the 5/8" angular brush for the ribbon, but you can also get the same results by using a flat brush. Always start on chisel edge, press the bristles to the side, pull back up on chisel edge.

Shade the skinny parts of your ribbon with **Green Mist** on tip and glaze in heel. Highlight the fat parts of your ribbon with **Titanium White** in tip and glaze in heel. (Tip: Use the **Green Mist** and **Titanium White** sparingly and blend very well before shading/highlighting.)

Twigs - Refer to Twigs Worksheet

Use watered down **Dark Chocolate** and the liner brush to paint the little twigs.

Shading Flesh

Use your #10 flat brush and base the outside and inside rim of this piece. Use two coats of **Shading Flesh**.

Finishing

Let your piece completely dry and seal with J.W. Wipe-On Varnish. Use a damp cloth and varnish to seal the piece.

I hope you enjoy painting this piece as much as I did!!

Pattern on Pullout

Chalk It Up With Roses
(Black Chalkboard)

Palette - DecoArt Americana

Black Green	Green Mist	Mint Julep Green	Avocado
French Mauve	Emperor's Gold	Cranberry Wine	Titanium White
Cadmium Yellow	Burnt Umber	Brush n' Blend	
Faux Glazing Medium			

Chalk it up with Roses continued
Brushes - Loew Cornell
    5/8" Angle   #10/0 Liner   #4 Filbert   #2 Round

Other Brushes
3/4" Scheewe Foliage Angular S8037   **Pattern on Pullout**

Other Supplies
    J.W. Etc. White Lightning   Blue Painters Tape
    Fine Sanding Block and Tack Cloth   J. W. Wipe on Varnish
    Graphite Paper   Blue Chalk Pencil
    Dunn-Edwards Acrylic Chalkboard Paint - Black
    Sponge Brush or Large Brush (for Chalkboard Paint)

Prep

Sand a 16" x 20" piece of Cedar Plywood until smooth to the touch. Use tack cloth to remove particles of wood and dust. Use a blue chalk pencil and make little marks all the way around the board approximately 2-3/4" inches from the outside of board. Use JW White Lightning and base the outside of the board. I use two coats, sanding lightly in between coats. Let dry.

Tape off the middle of the chalkboard so that the chalkboard paint does not bleed on to the White Lightning side. You will need to brush on at least two coats of chalkboard paint, sanding lightly between coats (refer to back of can).

Enough of this base coating stuff. Remove the tape and let's paint ☺!

Background Foilage

I use the Scheewe Foliage Angular to pounce a little background color. (*Tip: Let the brush sit in water for a couple of minutes before using. It will soften the bristles and make it easier to use*). Stipple the green colors in the order that they are listed in the palette list. Stipple where the roses and leaves are going to be painted, remembering to cover the edges just a little bit. This will soften the look of your completed piece.
(*Tip: Most of this stippling will be covered by roses, leaves and ribbon. Don't spend a lot of time worrying about this process*).

If you choose to use the patterns, trace them on at this point with graphite paper.

Roses - Refer to RoseWorksheet

I have put two colors of roses on this piece. I used **Cranberry Wine/Titanium White** on four of the roses and then **French Mauve/TitaniumWhite** on the other three. See picture of Rose Chalkboard.

Base in the shape of the rose using either of the above color combinations. I refer to the **Cranberry Rose** in the below instructions and on the Rose Worksheet. The **French Mauve** rose will be painted in the exact way. Let dry.

Let's paint roses. Using the 5/8" angular brush, dip the tip in **Titanium White** and the heel of the brush in **Cranberry Wine**. Blend and load until your brush is fully loaded ... about 3/4th way up your bristles...(*Tip: Dip and blend at least four times before you paint*).

Chalk it up with Roses continued

Use the Rose Worksheet as a guide. Start at the top…and while this is drying, skip down and do the sides and bottom. Come back and fill in the middle. *(Tip: If your brush starts to drag..dip it in just a little bit of Glaze, blend and paint again. After you paint a few roses, you will need to clean your brush and reload again).*

Buds - Refer to Rose Worksheet

Paint the buds first then use **Avocado** and the #2 round to paint and shape in the calyxes. Let dry and brush a little of the **Mint Julep Green** over the **Avocado**.

Leaves - Refer to Leaf Worksheet

Base the leaves with **Avocado** and **Black Green**.

Use **Mint Julep Green** to pull a vein from one end to the other end of the leaf with the chisel edge of my 5/8" angular brush. While the vein is wet, pull down some "feathers". Use the same brush and pull in **Mint Julep Green** from the outside toward the middle of the leaf.

Now, this is the fun part! I pulled in some of the **French Mauve** like I used in my roses. Pull in just like you did the **Mint Julep Green**. *(Tip: I pull in all kinds of colors depending on the colors I used in my project. This is my favorite part of painting a leaf.)*

Use your liner and thinned down **Titanium White** and **Mint Julep Green** and add veins to the leaves.

Use your liner and pull from the outside in and only on one side the **Emperor's Gold**.

Ribbon - Refer to RibbonWorksheet

Mix one part **Mint Julep Green** with four parts of Faux Glazing Medium.
(Tip: The glaze will make the ribbon look transparent.) Use a 5/8" angular brush for the ribbon. You can also get the same results by using a flat brush. Always start on chisel edge, press the bristles to the side, pull back up on chisel edge.

Shade the skinny parts of your ribbon with **Green Mist** on tip and glaze in heel. Highlight the fat parts of your ribbon with Titanium White in tip and glaze in heel.
*(Tip: Use the **Green Mist** and **Titanium White** sparingly and blend very well before shading/highlighting).*

Filler Flowers - Refer to Filler Flower Worksheet

Use a #4 Filbert and **Titanium White** to pull in these little filler flowers.

Twigs - Refer to Twig Worksheet

Use watered down **Burnt Umber** and the liner brush to paint the little twigs.
(Tip: As you are painting the twigs, roll your brush between your fingers….it will make the twigs look a little more realistic.)

Finishing

Let your piece completely dry and seal with J.W. Wipe-On Varnish. Use a damp cloth and varnish to seal my piece. DO NOT get this varnish on the chalkboard portion of your project.

Basket of Roses Mailbox

Palette - DecoArt Americana

Avocado	Burnt Umber	French Mauve	Black Green
Cadmium Yellow	Heritage Brick	Emperor's Gold	Green Mist
Light Buttermilk	Titanium White	Mint Julep Green	Blend n' Brush
Faux Glazing Medium			

Brushes - Loew Cornell

3/4", 5/8" Angular   #10/0 Liner
#16 , 1" Flat   #4 Filbert

Other Brushes

3/4" Scheewe Foliage Angular (S8037)

Other Supplies

Alcohol   Paper Towels
J.W. Exterior Varnish   Graphite Paper
Stylus   Large Sponge Brush
Metal Mailbox (Lowe's or Home Depot)

Prep

I love painting mailboxes…no prep!!! Just wipe w/alcohol, let dry and paint. There is a front and back on this piece... see pattern designs.

Basket

These baskets are so easy to paint. I use this same technique on all shapes of baskets. *(Tip: Use plenty of paint so that this basket will have texture when dry).* Basecoat the basket with **Burnt Umber** using the 1" flat brush. Use two coats…letting dry between coats. *(Tip: This basket will go through an ugly stage..don't panic☺.)* Use the #16 flat brush and **Light Buttermilk** to paint on the vertical lines on the basket. Stay on chisel edge and pull toward the bottom of the basket.

To paint the horizontal wicker lines, use the same dirty brush. Pick up **Light Buttermilk** on one side of the brush and **Burnt Umber** on the other. Start on chisel edge and pull from one side to the other (this blends the two colors together). Alternate the wicker lines…see pattern for placement. To tidy up the sides, turn your brush on a vertical angle and pull from the top toward the bottom.

After the basket is dry, pull **Emperor's Gold** through some of the basket…see photograph for placement.

Background Foliage

I don't spend a lot of time on the background foliage because I paint over most of it anyway☺. *(Tip: Let the foliage brush sit in water to soften the bristles. After the brush is soft, tap the background on the mailbox first, it gives it "tooth" so that the roses and*

**WILD ROSE BLOSSOMS
BLACK CHALKBOARD
PAGES 52 - 54
PULLOUT**

**WILD ROSE BLOSSOMS
VOTIVE CANDLE HOLDERS
PAGES 24 - 26**

Rose

Use White on tip and Cranberry Wine in heel. Pat in the bud shape.

Base in calyxes with Avocado. Let dry and brush a little Mint Julep Green over the Avocado.

To create thin branches. Use liner brush and thinned down Burnt Umber. Roll the liner brush between your fingers while pulling the brush.

Shadow leaves are made with glaze and left over color in brush.

Filler flowers are made with #4 filbert and White. Dots are Cadmium Yellow.

Mix Mint Julep Green with glaze. Use the 5/8" angle brush to paint ribbon. Start on chisel edge, lean the brush while pulling and end up on chisel edge.

Basket of Roses Mailbox - Background Foliage continued

such will adhere better). With a very light touch, tap the following in order: **Black Green**, **Avacodo**, **Mint Julep Green** and **Emperor's Gold**. (Refer to pattern.)

Roses - Refer to Rose Worksheet

Use a 5/8" angular shader and base the roses with **Heritage Brick**. Use **Light Buttermilk** on the tip and **Heritage Brick** on the heel.

See Rose Worksheet for the buds. Use **Cadmium Yellow** and your Stylus to make the small dots in the buds and roses.

Leaves - Refer to Leaf Worksheet

Base leaves with **Avocado** and **Black Green** using a 5/8" angular shader. Let dry.

Follow Leaf Worksheet to build the rest of the leaf. Use **Mint Julep Green** for the "feathers". Use **French Mauve** on the opposite side and pull toward the middle. Use **Mint Julep Green**, **TitaniumWhite** and water for the veins. Pull in **Emperor's Gold** on one side of the leaf.

Ribbon - Refer to Ribbon Worksheet

Mix one part **Green Mist** with four parts of Faux Glazing Medium. Use the 3/4" angular brush. Always start on chisel edge, press the bristles to the side, pull back up on chisel edge.

Shade the skinny parts of your ribbon with **Green Mist** on tip and glaze in heel. Highlight the fat parts of your ribbon with **Titanium White** in tip and glaze in heel.

Little White Highlights - Refer to Worksheet

Use **Titanium White** and pull in little filler flowers here and there.

Twigs - Refer to Worksheet

Use thinned down **Burnt Umber** and your liner brush to paint the twigs. *(Tip: Roll the brush between your fingers to make a more natural looking twig.)*

Finishing

Let your piece completely dry and seal with J.W. Exterior Varnish. I use a large damp sponge brush. I brush from side to side with a light touch. I seal with three coats of varnish, letting dry completely between applications. (Tip: This varnish will give texture to the mailbox…I love the way it looks and feels!)

Enjoy!

Pattern on Pullout

Decorative Rose Lamp

Palette - DecoArt Americana

Avocado	French Mauve	Emperor's Gold	Black Green
Cranberry Wine	Titanium White	Mint Julep Green	Cadmium Yellow
Green Mist	Brush'n Blend Medium		

Brushes - Loew Cornell

5/8" Angle   #10/0 Liner   #4 Filbert

Other Supplies

Graphite Paper   Stylus   Fabric Lamp Shade

Prep

No preparation. I love these no prep surfaces. If you choose to use the patterns, now is the time to trace them on. Use the graphite paper and the Stylus to lightly trace the pattern on the fabric shade.

Roses (Step #1) - Refer to Rose Worksheet

I have put two colors of roses on this piece. I used **Cranberry Wine/Titanium White** for one rose and then **French Mauve /Titanium White** on the other two.

I have found when painting on fabric, you need to put down a heavy basecoat before starting your rose. So when I paint fabric, I bounce around a lot because I hate waiting for paint to dry! Base in the roses and the rose buds using the colors listed. Let dry.

Leaves (Step #1) - Refer to Leaf Worksheet

I hate…hate…hate…waiting for paint to dry! Let's paint the leaves while we are waiting on the roses to dry. Base the leaves with **Avocado** and **Black Green**. At this time also put the calyxes around the buds. See Leaf Worksheet for shape and technique. I fit the leaves in and around the basecoated roses. Let dry and then we will come back and finish them.

Ribbon - Refer to Ribbon Worksheet

I usually mix one part **Mint Julep Green** with four parts of **Faux Glazing Medium**. *(Tip: The glaze will make the ribbon transparent, so adjust the color to your liking.)* Use a 5/8" angular brush for the ribbon. You can also get the same results by using a flat brush. Always start on chisel edge, press the bristles to the side, pull back up on chisel edge.

Shade the skinny parts of your ribbon with **Green Mist** on the tip and glaze in heel. Highlight the fat parts of your ribbon with **Titanium White** in tip and glaze in heel. *(Tip: Use the **Green Mist** and **Titanium White** sparingly and blend very well before shading/**Green Mist** and highlighting/**Titanium White**.)*

Decorative Rose Lamp continued
Roses (Step #2) - Refer to Rose Worksheet

Let's finish these roses☺ Using the 5/8" angular brush, dip the tip in **Titanium White** and the heel of the brush in **Cranberry Wine**. Blend and load until your brush is fully loaded….about 3/4th way up your bristles…*(Tip: I usually dip and blend at least four times before I'm ready to paint).*

Use the Rose Worksheet as a guide. Start at the top…and while the top strokes are drying, skip down and do the sides and bottom. Come back and fill in the middle. *(Tip: If your brush starts to drag…dip it in just a little bit of Brush'n Blend Medium, blend and paint again. After you paint a few roses, you will need to clean your brush and reload again.)*

Leaves (Step #2) - See Leaf Worksheet

Use **Mint Julep Green** to pull a vein from one end to the other end of the leaf with the chisel edge of a 5/8" angular brush. While the vein is wet, pull down some "feathers".

Use the same brush and pull in **Mint Julep Green** from the opposite side toward the middle. Let dry.

Here is the fun part! I pulled in some of the **French Mauve**. Pull in just like you did the **Mint Julep Green**. *(Tip: I pull in all kinds of colors depending on the colors I uses in my project...This is my favorite part of the painting a leaf.)* ☺

Use your liner and mix **Titanium White** and **Mint Julep Green** together and add veins to your leaf.

Use your liner and pull from the outside in and only on one side the **Emperor's Gold**. Do not thin the paint when painting these little accents on the leaf.

Filler Flowers - Refer to Filler Flower Worksheet

I use a #4 Filbert and **Titanium White** to pull in these little filler flowers.

Pattern on Pullout

Wild Rose Blossoms
(Black Chalkboard)

Palette - DecoArt Americana

Avocado	French Mauve	Emperor's Gold	Black Green
Titanium White	Antique Mauve	Hi-Lite Flesh	Cadmium Yellow
Burnt Umber	Mint Julep Green	Bosenberry Pink	Winter Blue
French Grey Blue	Brush n' Blend	Faux Glazing Medium	

Brushes - Loew Cornell

3/8", 5/8" Angular   #10/0 Liner   #6, #12 Flat   #2 Round

Other Supplies

J.W. Etc. White Lightning
Fine Sanding Block and Tack Cloth
J. W. Wipe on Varnish
Colored Chalk Pencil
Stylus
Dunn-Edwards Acrylic Chalkboard Paint - Black
Blue Painters Tape
Large Sponge Brush (for Chalkboard Paint)
Graphite Paper (Gray and White)
Ruler

Prep

Sand a 16" x 20" piece of Cedar Plywood until smooth to the touch. Use tack cloth to remove particles of wood and dust. Use a colored chalk pencil and make little marks all the way around the board approximately 2-3/4 inches from the outside of board. Use J.W. White Lightening and base the outside of the board. I use two coats, sanding lightly in between coats. Let dry.

Tape off the middle of the chalkboard so that the chalkboard paint does not bleed on to the White Lightening side. You will need to brush on at least two coats of chalkboard paint, sanding lightly between coats (refer to back of can). *(Tip: I use very little paint when I get close to the taped off area. You don't want the black chalkboard paint to seep under the tape.)* Let dry.

If you choose to use the patterns, trace them on at this point with graphite paper. *(Tip: You will use both black and white graphite paper depending on which area you are putting your pattern on.)* Do not trace all the small detail.

Let's paint☺

Wild Rose Blossoms - Refer to Wild Rose Blossom Worksheet

Use your #6 flat and base in all the blossoms with **Hi-Lite Flesh**. Let dry.

I randomly use both **Antique Mauve** and **Bosenberry Pink**. Paint all around the blossoms using these two colors. The color is on the tip of your 3/8" angular brush and **Brush n' Blend** on the heel. Let dry.

Wild Rose Blossoms - Refer to Wild Rose Blossom Worksheet

Use your liner and thinned down **Titanium White**, pull little white lines from the inside out. Do this on each petal.

Use your #2 round brush and **Cadmium Yellow** and dab a little yellow in the middle of each blossom. Let dry. Use your stylus and paint small dots with **Black Green**.

Use your #2 round and paint the white highlights on the tips of the petals. Use **TitaniumWhite** and fully load your brush. Start on chisel edge, press, and then come back up on chisel edge. *(Tip: I don't paint these on every petal.)*

Leaves - Refer to Leaf Worksheet

Base the leaves with **Avocado** and **Black Green**.

Use **Mint Julep Green** to pull a vein from one end to the other end of the leaf with the chisel edge of my 3/8" angular brush. While the vein is wet, pull down some "feathers".

Use the same brush and pull in **Mint Julep Green** from the outside in and let dry.

Now, this is the fun part! I pulled in some of the **French Mauve**. Pull in just like you did the **Mint Julep Green**. *(Tip: I pull in all kinds of colors depending on the colors I used in my project. This is my favorite part of painting a leaf.)* ☺

Use your liner and mix **Titanium White** and **Mint Julep Green** together and add veins to your leaf.

Use your liner and pull from the outside in and only on one side the **Emperor's Gold**. I do not thin the paint when I paint these little accents on the leaves.

Shadow Leaves - Refer to Shadow Leaves Worksheet

I mix **Faux Glazing Medium** with a little bit of **Mint Julep Green**. Use your #12 flat brush and make press leaves.

Ribbon - Refer to Ribbon Worksheet

I mixed one part **Winter Blue** with four parts of Faux Glazing Medium. *(Tip: The glaze will make the ribbon look transparent so adjust to your liking.)* Use a 5/8" angular brush for the ribbon, but you can also get the same results by using a flat brush. Always start on chisel edge, press the bristles to the side, pull back up on chisel edge.

Shade the skinny parts of your ribbon with **French Grey Blue** on tip and Faux Glazing Medium in the heel. Highlight the fat parts of your ribbon with **Titanium White** in tip and Faux Glazing Medium in the heel. Tip: (Use the **Winter Blue** and **French Grey Blue** sparingly and blend very well before shading/highlighting.)

Wild Rose Blossoms continued
Filler Berries - Refer to Berry Worksheet

I always have a pencil with an unused eraser or cotton swabs on my table. Use the end of the eraser or the cotton swabs to make these little berries. *(Tip: I use these little berries instead of filler flowers on a lot of projects.)* Dip into a little **Faux Glaze Medium** first, then dip into **Mint Julep Green**. *(Tip: Pounce a couple times before putting directly on your surface.)* Do this same technique and use **French Mauve**. Use your liner and thinned down **Titanium White** and put little dots in each berry.

Twigs - Refer to Twig Worksheet

I use watered down **Burnt Umber** and my liner brush to paint the little twigs. *(Tip: As you are painting the twigs, roll your brush between your fingers....it will make the twigs look a little more realistic.)*

Finishing

Let your piece completely dry and seal with J.W. Wipe-On Varnish. I use a damp cloth and varnish to seal my piece. DO NOT get this varnish on the chalkboard portion of your project.

I hope you enjoyed this project☺!

Pattern on Pullout

I hope you enjoyed the book!
Pam Childress
e-mail:
pamspaintedpretties2@yahoo.com

Susan Scheewe Publications Inc. 9-1-04

13435 N.E. Whitaker Way Portland, Or. 97230 PH (503) 254-9100   FAX (503) 252-9508   Orders Only (800) 796-1953

ACRYLIC BOOKS

Vol.	Title	#	Price
Vol. 2	"A Creative Brush" by Eileen Ackerson *NEW	569	$11.95
Vol. 1	"The Garden Path" by Sandi Brady Archer	492	$10.50
Vol. 1	"How Delicious" by Elaina Appleby *NEW	541	$10.50
Vol. 2	"Country Heartworks 2" by Reed Baxter	365	$10.50
Vol. 1	"The Flower Market" by Joyce Benner	319	$10.50
Vol. 3	"Acrylic Painting The Easy Way" by Bill Blackman	460	$10.50
Vol. 1	"Tole-tilly Tickled" by Lisa Brownie & Gina Knighton	490	$10.50
Vol. 3	"Country Fixin's - For All Seasons" by Rhonda Caldwell	332	$10.50
Vol. 1	"Country Celebration" by Tammy Christensen	378	$10.50
Vol. 1	"Folkart Friends" by Darcy Christensen	437	$10.50
Vol. 1	"Holly Berries and Twigs" by Kim Christmas *NEW	549	$10.50
Vol. 2	"Holly Berries and Twigs 2" by Kim Christmas *NEW	568	$11.95
Vol. 1	"A Beautiful Journey" by Linda & Michelle Coulter OIL & ACRYLIC *NEW	555	$10.50
Vol. 1	"Season's Change" by Susan Dircks DeWenter	551	$10.50
Vol. 2	"Season's Change 2" by Susan Dircks DeWenter *NEW	565	$11.95
Vol. 1	"A Painters Garden " by Jane Dillon	354	$10.50
Vol. 3	"A Painters Garden 3" by Jane Dillon	458	$10.50
Vol. 4	"A Painters Garden 4" by Jane Dillon	536	$10.50
Vol. 1	"Santas and Sams" by Bobi Dolara	258	$10.50
Vol. 2	"Vintage Peace" by Bobi Dolara	270	$10.50
Vol. 2	"Floral Designs 2" by Carol Empet	338	$10.50
Vol. 3	"Floral Portraits" by Carol Empet	358	$10.50
Vol. 1	"Angels Are Near" by Carol Freeman & Brenda Turley	375	$10.50
Vol. 2	"Briar Patch #2" by Sandy Fochler	424	$10.50
Vol. 3	"Briar Patch #3" by Sandy Fochler	456	$10.50
Vol. 4	"Briar Patch #4" by Sandy Fochler	479	$10.50
Vol. 5	"Briar Patch #5" by Sandy Fochler	506	$10.50
Vol. 1	"Between Friends-Briar Patch" by Sandy Fochler, Lorrie Dirksen, Holly Jespersen, Bonnie Morello	448	$10.50
Vol. 2	"Between Friends 2-Briar Patch" by Sandy Fochler, Lorrie Dirksen, Holly Jespersen, Bonnie Morello	473	$10.50
Vol. 2	"Deck The Halls Bauernmalerei" by Sherry Gall	391	$10.50
Vol. 1	"Pick of The Bunch" by Lola Gill	527	$10.50
Vol. 2	"Pick of The Bunch 2" by Lola Gill *NEW	559	$10.50
Vol. 1	"A Bear Necessity" by Denise Girling....CDA *NEW	550	$10.50
Vol. 1	"Giggles and Hugs" by Sandi Goodman *NEW	548	$10.50
Vol. 2	"Giggles and Hugs 2" by Sandi Goodman *NEW	564	$11.95
Vol. 1	"Olde Thyme Folk Art" by Teresa Gregory	390	$10.50
Vol. 1	"Maple Sugar" by Roberta Hall	444	$10.50
Vol. 3	"Maple Sugar 3" by Roberta Hall	471	$10.50
Vol. 4	"Maple Sugar 4" by Roberta Hall	481	$10.50
Vol. 5	"Maple Sugar 5" Country Jars by Roberta Hall	491	$10.50
Vol. 8	"Maple Sugar 8" by Roberta Hall	531	$10.50
Vol. 9	"Maple Sugar 9" by Roberta Hall	542	$10.50
Vol. 10	"Maple Sugar 10" by Roberta Hall *NEW	571	$11.95
Vol. 1	"Sunshine Kisses & Warm Winter Wishes" by Holly Hanley *NEW	560	$11.95
Vol. 1	"Endless Seasons" by Tiffany Hastie	498	$10.50
Vol. 1	"Endless Seasons 2" by Tiffany Hastie	521	$10.50
Vol. 1	"Garden Collection" by Bev Hink - Birdwell	526	$10.50
Vol. 1	"Artistic Treasures" by June Houck & Veda Parsley	535	$10.50
Vol. 2	"Artistic Treasures 2" by June Houck & Veda Parsley *NEW	535	$11.95
Vol. 1	"Happy Heart, Happy Home" by Cathy Jones	241	$10.50
Vol. 1	"Asako's Berry Hill Farm" by Asako Kan	515	$12.95
Vol. 2	"Asako's Berry Hill Farm 2" by Asako Kan	524	$10.50
Vol. 1	All Things Possible" by Susan Kelley	512	$10.50
Vol. 2	"All Things Possible 2" by Susan Kelley *NEW	544	$10.50
Vol. 2	"Dandelions 2" by Carla Kern	513	$10.50
Vol. 2	"Serendipity Collectibles" by Deborha Kerr	289	$10.50
Vol. 1	"Painted Memories, A Mother's Love" by Deborha Kerr	435	$10.50
Vol. 3	"Pickets & Pastimes 3, Feathered Inns" by M. & J. King	385	$10.50
Vol. 1	"For Me & My House" by Myrna King	370	$10.50
Vol. 1	"Enjoy The Seasons" By Roni LaBree	510	$12.95
Vol. 2	"Enjoy The Seasons 2" By Roni LaBree	538	$10.50
Vol. 3	"Enjoy The Seasons 3" By Roni LaBree	557	$10.50
Vol. 1	"Huckleberry Horse" by Hanna Long	269	$10.50
Vol. 2	"Country Favorites" by Hanna Long	489	$10.50
Vol. 3	"Country Favorites 2" by Hanna Long	514	$10.50
Vol. 2	"Love Lives Here" by Mary Lynn Lewis	185	$6.50
Vol. 3	"Love Lives Here" by Mary Lynn Lewis	195	$6.50
Vol. 1	"Everything Under The Moon" by Jackie Ludwig	421	$10.50
Vol. 1	"Second Nature" by Kathy McPherson	427	$10.50
Vol. 2	"Second Nature 2" by Kathy McPherson	463	$10.50
Vol. 6	"Special Welcomes #6 Crop Keepers" by Corinne Miller	347	$10.50
Vol. 4	"Bitterroot Backroads 4" by Glenice Moore	478	$10.50
Vol. 5	"Bitterroot Backroads 5 - Painting Birds" by Glenice Moore	487	$10.50
Vol. 6	"Bitterroot Backroads 6" by Glenice Moore	511	$10.50
Vol. 7	"Bitterroot Backroads 7" by Glenice Moore	540	$10.50
Vol. 8	"Bitterroot Backroads 8" by Glenice Moore *NEW	567	$11.95
Vol. 1	"Fruit & Flower Fantasies" by Joyce Morrison	277	$10.50
Vol. 2	"Fruit & Flower Fantasies 2" by Joyce Morrison	382	$10.50
Vol. 1	"Those Blooming Bears" by Cindy Ohama	493	$10.50
Vol. 4	"Those Blooming Bears 4" by Cindy Ohama *NEW	547	$10.50
Vol. 5	"Those Blooming Bears & More #5" by Cindy Ohama *NEW	562	$11.95
Vol. 1	"Whimsical Critters" by Lori Ohlson	228	$7.50
Vol. 1	"Sunflower Farm" by Lori Ohlson	326	$10.50
Vol. 1	"Seasons Delight" by Jurate Okura	500	$10
Vol. 2	"Season's Delight 2" by Jurate Okura	522	$10
Vol. 3	"Friends Forevermore 3 - Kitchen & More" by Karen Ortman	509	$1
Vol. 1	"Holiday Medley" by Nina Owens	265	$10
Vol. 2	"Another Holiday Medley" by Nina Owens	296	$10
Vol. 1	"Gifts & Graces" by Charlene Pena	475	$10
Vol. 2	"Gifts & Graces 2" by Charlene Pena	497	$10
Vol. 3	"Gifts & Graces 3" by Charlene Pena	534	$10
Vol. 3	"Tailfeathers 3" by Gisele Pope & Carla Kern	476	$10
Vol. 8	"Now & Then" by La Rae Parry	428	$10
Vol. 1	"Between The Vines" by Jamie Mills Price	400	$10
Vol. 2	"Between The Vines 2" by Jamie Mills Price	419	$10
Vol. 4	"Between The Vines 4" by Jamie Mills Price	474	$12
Vol. 1	"Forever In My Heart" by Diane Richards.....AC/Fabric	188	$6
Vol. 2	"Memories In My Heart" by Diane Richards.....AC/Fabric	189	$6
Vol. 3	"Forever In My Heart II" by Diane Richards.....AC/Fabric	205	$10
Vol. 7	"Nostalgic Dreams" by Diane Richards	273	$10
Vol. 8	"Heavenly Treasures" by Diane Richards	472	$10
Vol. 1	"Country Classics" by Karen Rideout	413	$10
Vol. 2	"Country Classics 2" by Karen Rideout	465	$10
Vol. 1	"Country Fun For Chistmas" by Tina Rodrigues	367	$10
Vol. 2	"Country Fun 2" by Tina Rodrigues	383	$10
Vol. 3	"Country At Heart" by Tina Rodrigues	401	$10
Vol. 4	"Country At Heart 4" by Tina Rodrigues	410	$10
Vol. 1	"Painting In The Spirit" by Jill Paris Rody	529	$10
Vol. 4	"Keepsake Sampler" by Susan & Camille Scheewe	200	$10
Vol. 1	"Schoolhouse Treasures" by Cathy Schmidt	408	$10
Vol. 2	"Schoolhouse Treasures" by Cathy Schmidt	433	$10
Vol. 3	"Schoolhouse Treasures 3 - Blackbird Inn" by Cathy Schmidt	518	$10
Vol. 1	"Holiday Hangarounds" by Marsha Sellers	327	$10
Vol. 1	"Huckleberry Friends" by Cheryl Seslar	393	$10
Vol. 2	"Huckleberry Friends 2" by Cheryl Seslar	403	$10
Vol. 3	"Huckleberry Friends 3" by Cheryl Seslar	431	$10
Vol. 1	"Kindred Hearts" by Viki Sherman	532	$10
Vol. 2	"Kindred Hearts 2 " by Viki Sherman *NEW	556	$10
Vol. 1	"Friendship Creek" by Katherine Smith	496	$10
Vol. 2	"Creations In Canvas...and More" by Carol Spooner	256	$10
Vol. 1	"Gran's Garden" by Ros Stallcup	295	$10.5
Vol. 2	"Another Gran's Garden" by Ros Stallcup	315	$10.5
Vol. 4	"Gran's Garden Party" by Ros Stallcup	345	$10.5
Vol. 5	"Gran's Treasures" by Ros Stallcup	363	$10.5
Vol. 10	"Gran's Magic-Bells, Books & Candles" by Ros Stallcup	466	$12.9
Vol. 11	"Gran" Attic" by Ros Stallcup	483	$12.9
Vol. 12	"Gran's Pantry" by Ros Stallcup	508	$12.9
Vol. 13	"Gran's Cottage" by Ros Stallcup	533	$12.9
Vol. 14	"Gran's Workbook" by Ros Stallcup *NEW	552	$12.9
Vol. 15	"Gran's Presents" by Ros Stallcup *NEW	570	$12.9
Vol. 1	"Storybook Lane - Harber Boy's Collection" by Sandy Starkel	520	$10.5
Vol. 2	"Blackberry Hollow" by Margaret Steed	407	$10.5
Vol. 1	"Keepsakes For The Holidays" by Charleen Stempel & S. Scheewe	286	$10.5
Vol. 1	"Christmas Greetings from the Cottage" by Chris Stokes	336	$10.5
Vol. 1	"Christmas Visions" by Max Terry	278	$10.5
Vol. 3	"Painting Clay Pot-pourri" by Max Terry	310	$10.5
Vol. 7	"Country Primitives 7" by Maxine Thomas	459	$10.5
Vol. 8	"Country Primitives 8" by Maxine Thomas	482	$10.5
Vol. 1	"Rise & Shine" by Jolene Thompson	214	$6.50
Vol. 2	"The Garden Gate" by Jolene Thompson	250	$10.50
Vol. 5	"Count Your Blessings" by Chris Thornton	213	$10.50
Vol. 6	"Share Your Blessings" by Chris Thornton	226	$10.50
Vol. 7	"Blessings" by Chris Thornton	255	$10.50
Vol. 9	"Blessings For The Home" by Chris Thornton	275	$10.50
Vol. 11	"Painted Blessings" by Chris Thornton	323	$10.50
Vol. 12	"Family Blessings" by Chris Thornton	349	$10.50
Vol. 15	"Multitude of Blessings" by Chris Thornton	379	$10.50
Vol. 17	"Blessings For The Home & Garden" by Chris Thornton	423	$12.95
Vol. 18	"Blessings To Treasure" by Chris Thornton	438	$10.50
Vol. 19	"Blessings To Share" by Chris Thornton	470	$10.50
Vol. 20	"Blessings In A Jar" by Chris Thornton	494	$10.50
Vol. 21	"Blessings In A Jar 2" by Chris Thornton	505	$10.50
Vol. 22	"Blessings In A Jar 3" by Chris Thornton *NEW	546	$10.50
Vol. 1	"Peasantries" by Mary Tiner *NEW	554	$10.50
Vol. 2	"Farmer and Friends" by Lou Ann Trice	366	$10.50
Vol. 3	"Jars, Jars, Jars!' 3" by Cindy Trombley *NEW	553	$10.50
Vol. 2	"Bears Inn Jars 2" by Paula Walsh *NEW	563	$11.95
Vol. 5	"Daydreams & Sweet Shirts II" by Don & Lynn Weed	208	$10.50
Vol. 1	"Pitter-Patter-Pigtail-Girls! A Simpler Thyme" by Stacy Gross West	432	$10.50
Vol. 2	"Country Doodles 2" by Amanda Williams	484	$10.50
Vol. 1	"All Of The Holidays" by Chris Williams	443	$10.50
Vol. 1	"Connie's Favorite Old-Time Labels" by Connie Williams	335	$10.50
Vol. 2	"Connie's Garden Seed Packets" by Connie Williams	351	$10.50
Vol. 1	"Floral Fabrics and Watercolor" by Sally Williams	262	$10.50
Vol. 1	"A Time For Giving" by Evelyn Wright	308	$10.50

Add $3.00 for one ...
Add $1.50 per each additional book. Please Add $4.00 for handling

Susan Scheewe Publications Inc.

9-1-04

13435 N.E. Whitaker Way Portland, Or. 97230 PH (503)254-9100 FAX (503)252-9508 Orders Only (800)796-1953

WATERCOLOR/ACRYLIC BOOKS

Vol.	Title	#	Price
Vol. 21	"Simply Watercolor" by Susan Scheewe Brown.....T.V. Book	260	$11.95 ___
Vol. 26	"Watercolor - The Garden Scene" by Susan Scheewe Brown... T.V. Book	339	$11.95 ___
	13-1/2 Hour Shows on 4 Videos. Video Library #8375 $69.99		
Vol. 27	"Watercolor Landscapes" by Susan Scheewe Brown....T.V. Book	360	$11.95 ___
	13-1/2 Hour Shows on 4 Videos. Video Library #8376 $69.99		
Vol. 28	"Watercolor - Garden Treasures" by Susan Scheewe Brown....T.V. Book	361	$11.95 ___
	13-1/2 Hour Shows on 4 Videos. Video Library #8377 $69.99		
Vol. 30	"Scheewe Art Workshop - Watercolor & Acrylic" by Susan Scheewe Brown..T.V. Bk.	398	$11.95 ___
	13-1/2 Hour Shows on 4 Videos. Video Library #8384 $69.99		
Vol. 31	"Enjoy Watercolor & Acrylic" by Susan Scheewe Brown.....T.V. Book	399	$11.95 ___
	13-1/2 Hour Shows on 4 Videos. Video Library #8385 $69.99		
Vol. 32	"Le Jardin" by Susan Scheewe Brown.....T.V. Book	414	$12.95 ___
	13-1/2 Hour Shows on 4 Videos. Video Library #8386 $69.99		
Vol. 33	"Simply Acrylic & Watercolor" by Susan Scheewe Brown.....T.V. Book	418	$12.95 ___
	13-1/2 Hour Shows on 4 Videos. Video Library #8387 $69.99		
Vol. 34	"A Paintbox of Ideas" Vol. 1 by Susan Scheewe Brown.....T.V. Book	442	$12.95 ___
	13-1/2 Hour Shows on 4 Videos. Video Library #8440 $69.99		
Vol. 35	"A Paintbox of Ideas" Vol. 2 by Susan Scheewe Brown.....T.V. Book	430	$12.95 ___
	13-1/2 Hour Shows on 4 Videos. Video Library #8441 $69.99		
Vol. 36	"Welcomes-A Paintbox of Ideas" Vol. 3 by Susan Scheewe Brown. .T.V. Book	445	$12.95 ___
	13-1/2 Hour Shows on 4 Videos. Video Library #8442 $69.99		
Vol. 37	"Paintbox Full of Animals" by Susan Scheewe Brown..T.V. Book	450	$12.95 ___
	13-1/2 Hour Shows on 4 Videos. Video Library #8443 $69.99		
Vol. 38	"Enjoy Acrylic" by Susan Scheewe Brown...T.V...Book	485	$12.95 ___
	13-1/2 Hour Shows on 4 Videos. Video Library #8452 $69.99		
Vol. 39	"Paintbox In The Garden" by Susan Scheewe Brown...T.V....Book	499	$12.95 ___
	13-1/2 Hour Shows on 4 Videos. Video Library #8456 $69.99		
Vol. 40	"Paintbox Full Of Greetings" by Susan Scheewe Brown...T.V....Book	504	$12.95 ___
	13-1/2 Hour Shows on 4 Videos. Video Library #8457 $69.99		
Vol. 41	"Along Country Roads" Acrylic & Watercolor by Susan Scheewe Brown...T.V....Book	525	$12.95 ___
	13-1/2 Hour Shows on 4 Videos. Video Library #8460 $69.99		
Vol. 42	"Gifts & Greetings" Acrylic & Watercolor by Susan Scheewe Brown...T.V....Book	528	$12.95 ___
	13-1/2 Hour Shows on 4 Videos. Video Library #8461 $69.99		
Vol. 43	"Beginning Watercolors" by Susan Scheewe Brown..........................*NEW*	545	$12.95 ___
	13-1/2 Hour Shows on 4 Videos. Video Library #8464 $69.99		
N Vol. 44	"Echoes of Nature" Acrylic by Susan Scheewe Brown.........................*NEW*..	558	$12.95 ___
	13-1/2 Hour Shows on 4 Videos. Video Library #8465 $69.99		
W Vol. 4	"Watercolor Made Easy 4" by Kathie George	453	$10.50 ___
Vol. 1	"Watercolor Fun & Easy" by Beverly Kaiser	243	$7.50 ___
Vol. 7	"Watercolor Charms" by Sharon Rachal	376	$10.50 ___

LOOK FOR US ON-LINE!

REACH OUR WEB SITE AT:
http://www.painting-books.com

e-mail us: SCHEEWEPUB@aol.com

NAME _____

_____

ADDRESS _____

_____

CITY/STATE/ZIP _____

_____

PH( ) _____

VISA _____

M/C _____

EXP.DATE _____

VIDEOS BY SUSAN SCHEEWE BROWN

Title	#	Price
"Watercolor Painting with Children" 1 Hour	S8222	$19.99 ___
"Paintbox In My Garden" 1 Hour	S8379	$19.99 ___
"Watercolor Techniques" 1 Hour	S8226	$19.99 ___
"Painting Projects" Watercolor 3 Hours...Trees and Leaves	S8224	$49.99 ___
"Acrylic Techniques For Everyone" 1 Hour	S8368	$19.99 ___
"Watercolor Painting" Problems & Solutions 1 Hour	S8232	$19.99 ___
"Acrylic Painting" Problems & Solutions 1 Hour	S8233	$19.99 ___

PEN & INK BOOKS / COLORED PENCIL BOOKS

Vol.	Title	#	Price
Vol. 6	"Journey of Memories" by Claudia Nice	166	$6.50 ___
Vol. 2	"Colored Pencil Made Easy" by Jane Wunder	242	$7.50 ___
Vol. 4	"Watercolor, Pen and Ink" by Jane Wunder	357	$10.50 ___

OILS BOOKS

Vol.	Title	#	Price
Vol. 7	"Paint 'n Patch" by Susan Scheewe	107	$5.50 ___
Vol. 11	"I Love To Paint" by Susan Scheewe	111	$6.50 ___
Vol. 2	"Western Images 2" by Becky Anthony	436	$10.50 ___
Vol. 10	"Flower Show" by Georgia Bartlett	415	$10.50 ___
Vol. 4	"Countryscapes" by Donna Bell	249	$10.50 ___
Vol. 5	"Painter to Painter" by Donna Bell	263	$10.50 ___
Vol. 3	"Acrylic Painting Made Easy" by Bill Blackman	460	$10.50 ___
Vol. 2	"Mini Mini More" by Terri and Nancy Brown	151	$6.50 ___
Vol. 4	"Heritage Trails" by Terri and Nancy Brown	169	$6.50 ___
Vol. 6	"Windows of My World 6" by Jackie Claflin	464	$10.50 ___
Vol. 7	"Windows of My World 7" by Jackie Claflin	507	$10.50 ___
Vol. 8	"Windows of My World 8' by Jackie Claflin............*NEW*..	561	$11.95 ___
Vol. 1	"A Beautiful Journey" by Linda & Michelle Coulter OIL & ACRYLIC.*NEW*	555	$10.50 ___
Vol. 1	"Expressions In Oil" by Delores Egger	154	$6.50 ___
Vol. 2	"Days of Heaven" by Gloria Gaffney	252	$10.50 ___
Vol. 6	"The Sky's The Limit" by Jean Green	372	$10.50 ___
Vol. 3	"Nature's Beauty" by Bill Huffaker	177	$6.50 ___
Vol. 1	"Ducks and Geese" by Jean Lyles	172	$6.50 ___
Vol. 2	"Another Path To Follow" by Lee McGowen	328	$10.50 ___
Vol. 2	"Bitterroot Backroads 2" by Glenice Moore	340	$10.50 ___
Vol. 4	"Bitterroot Backroads 4" by Glenice Moore. ACRYLIC	478	$10.50 ___
Vol. 5	"Bitterroot Backroads 5" by Glenice Moore. ACRYLIC	487	$10.50 ___
Vol. 1	"Stepping Stones" by Judy Nutter	121	$6.50 ___
Vol. 1	"Painting with Paulson" by Buck Paulson	343	$11.95 ___
Vol. 1	"Painting Flowers With Augie" by Augie Reis	152	$6.50 ___
Vol. 1	"Seascapes - Step by Step" by Rick Scott	488	$10.50 ___
Vol. 1	"Fantasy Folk" by Don Weed	123	$6.50 ___
Vol. 2	"Friends Are Forever" by Gene Waggoner	231	$10.50 ___
Vol. 3	"Creative Path" by Diane Nielsen Wallace	530	$10.50 ___
Vol. 1	"Something Special For Everyone" by Mildred Yeiser	158	$6.50 ___
Vol. 5	"Soft & Gentle Paintings" by Mildred Yeiser	268	$10.50 ___

SHIPPING & HANDLING CHARGES - U.S CURRENCY ONLY
Add $3.00 for the First Book for shipping and handling.
Add $1.50 per each additional book.
Please Add $4.00 for handling & postage. PER TAPES.
Sorry we must have a "NO REFUND - NO RETURN" policy.